MANAGING INSTITUTIONAL
SELF-STUDY

Managing Universities and Colleges: Guides to Good Practice

Series editors:

David Warner, Principal and Chief Executive, Swansea Institute of Higher Education

David Palfreyman, Bursar and Fellow, New College, Oxford

This series has been commissioned in order to provide systematic analysis of the major areas of the management of colleges and universities, emphasizing good practice.

Current and forthcoming titles include

Frank Albrighton and Julia Thomas (eds): *Managing External Relations*
Allan Bolton: *Managing the Academic Unit*
Robert W. Bushaway: *Managing Research*
Ann Edworthy: *Managing Stress*
Judith Elkin and Derek Law (eds): *Managing Information*
John M. Gledhill: *Managing Students*
Alison Hall: *Managing People*
Christine Humfrey: *Managing International Students*
Colleen Liston: *Managing Quality and Standards*
Patricia Partington and Caroline Stainton: *Managing Staff Development*
Harold Thomas: *Managing Financial Resources*
David Warner and David Palfreyman (eds): *Managing Crisis*
David Watson: *Managing Strategy*
David Watson and Elizabeth Maddison: *Managing Institutional Self-study*

MANAGING INSTITUTIONAL SELF-STUDY

David Watson and Elizabeth Maddison

Open University Press

Open University Press
McGraw-Hill Education
McGraw-Hill House
Shoppenhangers Road
Maidenhead
Berkshire
England
SL6 2QL

email: enquiries@openup.co.uk
world wide web: www.openup.co.uk

and Two Penn Plaza, New York, NY 10121–2289, USA

First published 2005

A catalogue record of this book is available from the British Library

ISBN-13: 978 0335 21502 7 (pb) 978 0335 21503 4 (hb)

ISBN-10: 0 335 21502 5 (pb) 0 335 21503 3 (hb)

Library of Congress Cataloguing-in-Publication Data
CIP data applied for

Typeset by YHT Ltd, London
Printed in Great Britain by MPG Books Ltd, Bodmin, Cornwall

CONTENTS

For Jacob

LIST OF FIGURES AND TABLES

FOREWORD

In the later months of 1993, the Higher Education Statistics Agency (HESA) was in the early stages of defining the data which it would collect from all higher education institutions in the United Kingdom in order to set in place the first UK-wide information system for higher education. On one day, as its Chief Executive, I received extremely angry letters from Vice-Chancellors of two major universities. One of them berated me in the strongest terms for imposing on institutions 'the most intolerable burdens' in respect of the collection of data about institutional finance, and observed that 'detailed financial data is a matter for the University and the University alone'. The other Vice-Chancellor accused me of 'suppressing important information of valid public interest', and urged that the financial data to be collected and analysed by HESA 'should be significantly extended to enable this university and others to compare themselves and their performance across the sector'. In the event, the two letters led to no change in the modest plans for data collection in respect of finance; but they do exemplify the tensions which exist in any consideration of performance measurement.

This book is about 'institutional self-study', as applied to universities and other higher education institutions. Within it, the authors have admirably related the theory of institutional self-study – or 'reflective practice' as they redefine it – to the practical planning and management of higher education institutions, and the dilemma generated by, on the one hand, the need for comparative information to help in policy formulation and, on the other, the rapidly changing and increasingly competitive climate in which UK higher education institutions are now operating.

Throughout the book, the importance, and the potential pitfalls, of evidence-based policy making are explored, and the lessons to be learned from previous experience are set out. The book charts the increasing influence of data and information on institutional planning and decision-making; and in the process the authors valuably differentiate data and information, and draw attention to the ways in which information can be both used and misused.

But it is the construction and description – though in no sense prescription – of a model of effective 'reflective practice' that forms the most valuable component of this important work. The book takes self-study to be a highly practical activity, embedded in a complex theoretical and political context. The authors have used their own institution, the University of Brighton, as a case study, even to the extent of including quite detailed comparative analyses. The insights into the data, planning and quality cycles of the University of Brighton are fascinating: and demonstrate both why Brighton has thrived since its designation as a university in 1992 and why the authors of this study have the confidence to publish so much institution-specific information.

In this book, the authors have drawn on their extensive experience to provide an invaluable perspective on institutional self-study that brings together both the theoretical and the practical aspects, and places them in a political context. In doing so, they provide a basis for other institutions to consider their own processes, but they also set out a challenge which will face the higher education sector in the United Kingdom in the future – how will institutions create an authentic account of themselves, to inform their potential students, their funding bodies, and most importantly themselves?

Brian Ramsden
Founding Chief Executive
Higher Education Statistics Agency

SERIES EDITORS'
INTRODUCTION

■

Post-secondary educational institutions can be viewed from a variety of different perspectives. For most of the students and staff who work in them they are centres of learning and teaching in which the participants are there by choice and consequently, by and large, work very hard. Research has always been important in some higher education institutions, but in recent years this emphasis has grown, and what for many was a great pleasure and, indeed, a treat, is becoming more of a threat and an insatiable performance indicator, which just has to be met. Maintaining the correct balance between quality research and learning/teaching, while the unit of resource, at best, holds steady, is one of the key issues facing us all. Educational institutions as work places must be positive and not negative environments.

From another aspect, post-secondary educational institutions are clearly communities, functioning to all intents and purposes like small towns and internally requiring and providing a similar range of services, while also having very specialist needs. From yet another, they are seen as external suppliers of services to industry, commerce and the professions. These 'customers' receive, *inter alia*: a continuing flow of well qualified, fresh graduates with transferable skills; part-time and short course study opportunities through which to develop existing employees; consultancy services to solve problems and help expand business; and research and development support to create new breakthroughs. It is an unwise UK educational institution that ignores this aspect, which is now given a very high priority by the UK government.

However, educational institutions are also significant businesses in their own right. One recent study shows that higher education institutions alone are worth £35 billion a year to the UK economy. Moreover, they create more than 562,000 full-time equivalent jobs either through direct employment or 'knock-on' effects. This is equivalent to 2.7 per cent of the UK workforce. In addition, it has recently been realized that UK higher education is a major export industry with the added benefit of long-term financial and political returns. If the UK further education sector is also added to this equation, then the economic impact of post-secondary education is of truly startling proportions.

Whatever perspective you take, it is obvious that educational institutions require managing and, consequently, this series has been produced to facilitate that end. The series editors have striven to identify authors who are distinguished practitioners in their own right and, indeed, can also write. The authors have been given the challenge of producing essentially practical handbooks, which combine appropriate theory and contextual material with many examples of good practice and guidance.

The topics chosen are both of key importance to educational management and stand at the forefront of current debate. Some of these topics have never been covered in depth before and all of them are equally applicable to further as well as higher education. The editors are firmly of the belief that the UK distinction between these sectors will continue to blur and will be replaced, as in many other countries, by a continuum where the management issues are entirely common.

For more than twenty years, both of the series editors were involved with a management development programme for senior staff from HEIs throughout the world. Every year the participants quickly learnt that we share the same problems and that similar solutions are normally applicable. Political and cultural differences may on occasion be important, but are often no more than an overlying veneer. Hence, this series will be of considerable relevance and value to post-secondary educational managers throughout the world.

One of the most successful volumes in this series has proved to be David Watson's *Managing Strategy*. Sir David, and his co-author Elizabeth Maddison, have now taken some of the themes of that book and explained in detail exactly how they can be put into practice through the means of institutional self-study. David and Elizabeth have carefully illustrated the theory with copious examples derived from their home institution, the University of Brighton. This focus upon a single institution does not irritate the reader because it is in no way a eulogy; rather it facilitates a much greater level of understanding and, at least in the case of the series editors, substantial envy.

It behoves all educational managers to be aware of the tool of institutional self-study and, wherever possible, to adopt it. Clearly, this *can* be achieved because, as the authors themselves point out, they are actually doing the job at the same time as they have written about it.

David Warner
David Palfreyman

ACKNOWLEDGEMENTS

Our collaboration on this book weaves together a number of strands. Its main subject constitutes a large part of our day jobs, and in attempting to understand how institutional self-study really works we have learned from and been supported by numerous colleagues at the University of Brighton. At the same time we have allowed this obsession to leak into various of our extra-curricular or night jobs, and have also benefited from the insights of colleagues in other institutions, notably members of the Longer Term Strategy Group of Universities UK and the planning network of the Association of University Administrators. Earlier drafts of parts of the book have also turned up in unlikely places, such as the annual series of lectures on higher education sponsored by Green College Oxford and a postgraduate dissertation at the University of Warwick. We are grateful to the University of the West of England for permission to use Figure 6.2, and to Azure Consulting International for permission to use Figure 9.3.

Round the final lap, the full manuscript was read and commented upon by the following friends: Rachel Bowden, David House, Sharon Jones, Stuart Laing and Brian Ramsden. Their advice was sound, clear and productively inconsistent. They also tried to save us from errors of fact and interpretation, and all of those which remain are entirely our own responsibility.

Doing the job and writing about it at the same time leads to regular breaches of the European Working Time Directive, and of otherwise humane and sensible institutional policies on work–life balance. We are grateful to our families for their tolerance, and in particular to Betty Skolnick and Kate Aughterson for their efforts to understand why we were doing this. Sarah West performed technical miracles at entirely unreasonable speed in preparing a complex manuscript, and Linda Miles found even more errors at the last minute. Our commissioning editor, Shona Mullen, quizzed us hard about how the book was going to work, and then sensibly left us alone.

LIST OF ABBREVIATIONS

ADC	Academic Development Committee
AIR	Association for Institutional Research
ASB	Adjusted Sector Benchmark
BNQP	Baldrige National Quality Program
BRRG	Better Regulation Review Group
BRTF	Better Regulation Task Force
CBI	Confederation of British Industry
CMU	Coalition of Mainstream Universities
CNAA	Council for National Academic Awards
CRE	Commission for Racial Equality
CUC	Committee of University Chairmen
DoH	Department of Health
DLHE	Destinations of Leavers from Higher Education
DTI	Department of Trade and Industry
EAIR	European Association for Institutional Research
EBPP	Evidence Based Policy and Practice Co-ordinating Centre
EFQM	European Framework for Quality Management
ESRC	Economic and Social Research Council
EUA	European University Association
FDTL	Fund for the Development of Teaching and Learning
FEC	full economic costing
FHEQ	Framework for Higher Education Quality
HE	higher education
HEFCE	Higher Education Funding Council for England
HEI	higher education institution
HEIF	Higher Education Innovation Fund
HEPI	Higher Education Policy Institute

HEQC	Higher Education Quality Council
HERO	Higher Education & Research Opportunities in the United Kingdom
HEROBAC	Higher Education Reach-out to Business and the Community
HESA	Higher Education Statistics Agency
HESES	Higher Education Students Early Statistics
ICT	Information and Communication Technologies
IoD	Institute of Directors
LTSN	Learning and Teaching Support Network
MIS	management information system(s)
NAO	National Audit Office
NCE	National Commission on Education
NCIHE	National Committee of Inquiry into Higher Education (also known as the Dearing Committee)
NSS	National Student Survey
OECD	Organization for Economic Cooperation and Development
Ofsted	Office for Standards in Education
OPM	Office for Public Management
OST	Office of Science and Technology
PIs	performance indicators
QAA	Quality Assurance Agency for Higher Education
RAE	Research Assessment Exercise
SCOP	Standing Conference of Principals
SED	self-evaluation document
SFCFHE	Scottish Funding Councils for Further and Higher Education
TAFE	technical and further education
TQA	teaching quality assessment
TQI	teaching quality information
TRAC	Transparency Review of Costing
TTA	Teacher Training Agency
UCAS	Universities and Colleges Admissions Service
UUK	Universities UK
VFM	value for money

PART 1 AN INTRODUCTION TO INSTITUTIONAL SELF-STUDY

1

SELF-STUDY AND ORGANIZATIONAL LEARNING

This book is about a special example of organizational learning which we have called institutional self-study: learning by, about and for the university. This chapter introduces the concept and its implications for higher education institutions (HEIs).

The theory and practice of organizational learning

The notion that the ability of an organization to learn – and to act on that learning – is directly related to long-term survival and success has become something of a mantra in recent writing about strategy in the private sector. At the simplest level there is the observation that 'since institutions have to adapt they have to learn' (Heywood 2000: 77). Bolder commentators see a learning or knowledge-based organization as having an immediate economic edge, as existing knowledge is magically (or systematically) transformed into new knowledge that gains market advantage (see Choo 1998; Davenport and Prusak 2000). For some, formal systems of knowledge management (often with a strongly held view about Japanese superiority in this field) help in converting tacit to explicit knowledge (Nonaka and Takeuchi 1995; Kidd 2002). Writers range from the evangelical (Garratt – for whom the learning organization is ideologically driven and should in turn drive strategy and structure towards a more democratic workplace [Garratt 2001]) to the coolly academic (Hodgkinson and Sparrow – for whom established principles of cognition and behavioural theory should inform our understanding of organizational strategy [Hodgkinson and Sparrow 2002]). Much of this terrain is helpfully – and influentially – mapped by Argyris (1999).

There are five lessons here for self-study. First, we should not be seduced by a simplistic model of organizational learning or the learning organization: 'the notion that a set of universalistic trends and competitive pressures is impelling organisations towards competition based on organisational learning is seriously flawed' (Keep and Rainbird 2002: 79). 'The notion of organizational learning is finally a reductive and idealistic metaphor. It too easily trivialises organizational change' (Whittington 1993: 128). It can also make the flawed assumption that organizations are rational, eliminating the 'residual equivocality [which] provides the necessary room for learning and adaptation' (Choo 1998: 261). It is also, importantly, 'no panacea' (Mintzberg *et al.* 1998: 228). Meanwhile, there may simply be an inherent and unbridgeable contradiction between notions of learning (implying increasing variety) and of organization (implying rules and processes that aim to reduce variety to what is manageable) (Hodgkinson and Sparrow 2002).

Secondly, and while exercising caution about some of these bolder claims, we should not ignore a series of interesting case studies apparently showing positive effects from a commitment to collective learning and to understand learning as a key to successful strategy. These include:

- deliberate efforts to change organizational culture, structure and practice (Shell [before its recent difficulties about the level of its reserves], or Ford, described by Choo 1998);
- the particular challenges of tackling organizational learning in organizations whose business is intangible (for example, probing the question of whether or not 'knowledge work' requires different organizational principles and practices, such as 'knowledge webs' [Miles *et al.* 2002: 348]);
- tightly circumscribed projects aiming to introduce a technical element to specific points of learning and decision-making (for example, decision-making heuristics in the health service [Milner 2000]); and
- conscious effort to develop and manage the ability to scan the environment as part of managing the organization's intangible assets (Pettigrew and Whipp 1991).

However, relatively few studies address how this applies in the public sector and fewer still in a university. Those that do range from the simplistic (Sallis and Jones [2002], on managing knowledge in education) to the sophisticated but sceptical (such as Fuller [2002], who doubts the capacity of universities to absorb the lessons of organizational learning in any meaningful way). Most helpful is the reminder that doing this well is above all about people (not technology), and that it requires a sensitive and mature understanding of organizational dynamics (Milner 2000). Duke takes this into the heart of the university 'as a particular institution and an organisational species' to focus on managing 'the tensions between continuity and change', to ask whether it is possible to manage the 'learning university' (Duke 2002: 3 and 7).

Thirdly, and on a practical level, self-study must generate signals which are then heeded. Otherwise, 'red light behaviour' results. This can occur, for example, when decisions are made in a context where 'the rational element points in a different direction to the emotional element' (Wissema 2002: 523–4). This comprises 'not noticing, ignoring, suppressing or scorning warning signals which, if properly addressed, would have contributed to preventing an incorrect decision' and, if repeated, results 'in a cycle of calamities of increasing impact' (Wissema 2002: 522). Fortunately, those that notice the signals, after having first passed them by, should thereby be capable of learning. To increase sensitivity to, and reduce the likelihood of missing, relevant signals, Wissema advocates technical and behavioural remedies, as well as 'adding significant reference points for decision making' (Wissema 2002: 537). Scott, *apropos* higher education, advocates decent management information systems as a prerequisite to avoiding crises (Scott 2003: 170).

Fourthly, 'it is obvious to anyone who has ever worked in an organization for a prolonged period that they continually make mistakes over and over again' (Rosenfield and Wilson 1999: 536). Self-study can thus help to avoid unnecessary learning (Mintzberg *et al.* 1998: 228). Unlearning is also sometimes as important as learning: 'the collective self-reinforcing nature of existing recipes requires that both learning and unlearning processes should extend deep into the organization' (Whittington 1993: 127).

Finally, self-study is fundamental to organizational competence (Choo 1998) and the capability of strategic foresight (Hodgkinson and Sparrow 2002). These notions eschew the bolder claims – and arguably the sterile debate – about organizational learning and the learning organization. They strike a chord with our definition in this work of self-study as 'collective reflective practice', and they advocate grounding an approach in the specific culture of the organization. Organizations can 'use information to construct meaning, create knowledge, and make decisions' (Choo 1998: 231). Strategic knowledge needs to be distributed throughout the organization, perhaps via 'knowledge elicitation techniques', while avoiding the impact of weaknesses in information handling 'that frequently undermine the strategy process' (Hodgkinson and Sparrow 2002: 295 and 308). This is not a quick fix – energy needs to be sustained, along with attention to developing competence, in a 'long-term, cumulative, progressive synthesis' (Pettigrew and Whipp 1991: 294).

Self-study and the university: definitions

Self-study is about collective reflective practice carried out by a university with the intention of understanding better and improving its own progress towards its objectives, enhancing its institutional effectiveness, and both responding to and influencing positively the context in which it is operating. As such, self-study is intimately linked to university strategy, culture and decision-making – with an emphasis on each of the collective, reflective and practical components of this definition. It is conceptually distinct from the related field of higher education research, in that it is directly undertaken to influence action. In terms of the distinction established by Malcolm and Zukas (2001), it is concerned to be 'for' rather than just 'about' higher education.

University self-study therefore requires a systematic and systemic approach to information collection and analysis and potentially covers all aspects of the university that pertain to mission, performance, decision-making and strategic change (Kells 1992; Slovacek 1988). It has a strong technical or practical component – how to measure and assess progress towards objectives and how to evaluate effectiveness. While its focus is predominantly internal, it must draw on external indicators, must reflect the external context and may involve external review: it is not about 'complete introspection' (Jamieson 1988: 125).

Meanwhile, self-study also has a vital political dimension. Part of this derives from the culture and position of the individual university and its preparedness to act on what it finds – the ability to embrace change. Another part is intimately linked to the peculiar culture of higher education. In this context, 'effective self-evaluation is crucial to a healthy self-regulating HE system' (Jackson and Lund 2000: 218). Self-study is a serious use of institutional energy and attention, expressing its responsibility as a self-governing community, or of 'the intrinsic nature of what it means to be an IHE [institution of higher education]' related to the 'hermeneutic conception of purposes' of a university (Barnett 1992: 93). 'Self-evaluation is fundamental to the notion of self-regulation. It is also integral to the management of change, improving the learning capacity of organisations and so enabling them to respond to change more effectively' (Jackson 1997: 73).

This makes self-study broader than collective or UK-wide quality assurance, albeit related to it. Quality assurance takes place under a nationally agreed framework; is subject to highly charged debate; and is focused on the institution being able to satisfy external expectations and standards about the awards it makes. Self-study arguably underpins the capacity to meet quality assurance requirements but aims at the delivery of overall institutional strategic performance rather than simply assurance of the academic awards made. As a recent report on the accountability burden endured by UK HEIs notes: 'from the institutions' side, continued refinement of corporate governance, control and information systems, benchmarked against best practice against other sectors and countries, will strengthen their arguments for greater self-regulation of their publicly-funded activities' (PA Consulting 2004b: 2). This kind of defensive or pre-emptive thinking is never far from the minds of institutional managers, however disappointing the results may be.

As set out in Part 2, self-study is thus more important the greater the emphasis placed by the community, its clients and other stakeholders on external measures of performance.

Self-study as defined here is better articulated in the US – often using the language of 'institutional research' – than in the UK (Jackson 2003). Two influential US definitions of institutional research offer us the following:

> An attitude of critical appraisal of all aspects of higher education, which has as its primary purpose the assessment and evaluation of the expressed goals of the institution and the means to achieve these goals.
>
> (Suslow 1971: 1)

> Research conducted within an institution of higher education to provide information which supports institutional planning, policy formation and decision making.
>
> (Saupe 1990: 6)

Towards reflective practice

There is, of course, a heady mixture of motives and aspirations going on here. The simple philosophical injunction 'know thyself' has always had its ambiguities, not least when it morphs (as it will in this book) into 'see yourself as others see you'. As Guy Browning comments in his *Guardian* column, 'It's actually a lot easier to study the great thinkers who said know thyself than it is to go the effort of actually knowing oneself. There are no study guides to oneself [until now], although hearing what your ex-partners say behind your back can be useful' (Browning 2004).

Three decades ago in the UK 'running' a university or college (there was no such thing as 'managing' such a delicate organism) was regarded as a matter of common sense. In universities the 'big jobs' were done by temporarily assigned senior academics and the Registrar as head of the administration; in the 'public sector,' such was the extent of local authority (and later central government) control that there were really no 'big jobs' at all. All of that has changed, as a result initially of two wake-up calls (although they felt more like being tipped out of bed). In the public sector the James Report of 1972, formally about teacher education, in fact swept the sector into a frenzy of reorganization; a decade later the universities reeled under the effect of Keith Joseph's radical cuts in funding.

Since then, simply 'keeping the show on the road' has not been an option for British institutional leaders. Knowing as much as possible about your own institution, its strengths and weaknesses, as well as its prospects and potentialities, has become a vital instrument of strategic management. As Browning might suggest, the motives here are mixed. They include the defensive (keeping the regulators off our backs); the self-interested (improving our competitive position); and the professional (achieving the self-respect that comes with improved performance).

Above all, those taking responsibility for self-study in a university need constantly to remember that a university is only a single or cohesive organism for certain purposes: to maintain a more or less distinctive mission; to create both the economic and the moral conditions in which staff and students can work safely and securely; and (as myriad examples here will show) to be accountable to others (chiefly funders). Beyond this, a university is in fact an alliance of separable communities: of subjects, disciplines and professions; of knowledge-generating and of supporting functions; and of individuals who may spend only a part of an otherwise coherent 'academic' career working within (and ideally for) it. Many of these alliances will also transcend the boundaries between it and other institutions, whether in the same (other universities and colleges) or different (industrial, commercial, governmental and public service) businesses. It's an unwise university leader who forgets that his or her institution is both inescapably flat in organization and professionally argumentative.

In preparing this book, we asked colleagues at Brighton to reflect on how useful self-study is to them in leading and managing the university. We also asked colleagues in other universities how they were currently approaching some of the issues implicit in self-study efforts. Like the respondents from other universities quoted in Chapter 2, we found within Brighton a general consensus that the need for good self-study is increasing: 'if we're not more systematic, significant change will be by luck not judgement' (SMT – member of the Senior Management Team).

Our colleagues were also critical of aspects of current practice, and warned about naïve optimism.

• They argued strongly for more and better information, without resorting to 'management by numbers': 'There is a danger that we get hooked in to routine consideration of quantifiable things and don't actually ask ourselves the more interesting and difficult questions about what makes performance change and improve' (SMT); 'Better information on costs would allow me to make investment decisions: I want a model of inputs and outputs' (D – Dean).

• They wanted to make more systematic use of information in decision-making, but not to work in a data-dependent culture: 'there's a balance between how much information you use and swamping people' (SA – School Administrator); 'In certain circumstances, more thinking and less research ... enough research, start thinking' (SMT).

• They had clear views about where responsibility for this work lay – or should lie: 'I expect [my senior staff] to do their jobs and essentially to own the information ... because (a) you've got to trust someone and (b) I would just drown otherwise' (SA); 'An awful lot of this stuff about how well a university does is down to the people in it and the climate and the culture ... There's a temptation ... that performance monitoring information is seen as the responsibility of people like you and me and that's exactly the wrong place to have it' (SMT).

• They wanted to be able to make better comparisons with other universities: 'self-study leading to comparative learning ... is [a feature] that the system as a whole has not really addressed so you get brittle and naive stuff about disseminating good practice ... lots of banal guides that nobody reads' (SMT); 'It's important to benchmark externally – that is the student's focus' (HS – Head of School); 'It's easier to compare research externally than internally because of subject cultures and different regimes' (HS).

• They understood clearly the complexity of the relationship between self-study and decision-making: 'Having a culture of reflectiveness ... is not always the same as having a very good understanding in information terms about what is going on inside the institution and how it fits into the bigger context ... if done in the wrong way each could be inimical to each other' (SMT).

These counsels against theoretical perfection are very much in the mould of responsible pragmatism. They thus contribute to a proud philosophical tradition. Writing in 1914, with Europe on the brink of chaos and in America the 'progressive' ideal running into the sand, the American political philosopher Walter Lippmann set out a manifesto for a careful, determined, scientific, non-dogmatic approach to social and political problems:

All we can do is to search the world as we find it, extricate the forces that seem to move it, and surround them with criticism and suggestion. Such a vision will inevitably reveal the bias of its author; that is to say it will be a human hypothesis not an oracular revelation. But if the hypothesis is honest and alive it should cast a little light upon our chaos. It should help us to cease revolving in the mere routine of the present or floating in a private utopia. For a vision of latent hope would be woven of vigorous strands; it would be concentrated on the crucial points of contemporary life, on that living zone where the present is passing into the future. It is the region where thought and action count. Too far ahead there is nothing but your dream; just behind there is nothing but your memory. But in the unfolding present, man can be creative if his vision is gathered from the promise of actual things.

(Lippmann 1914: 18)

Lippmann's book was called 'Drift and Mastery'. 'Vision gathered from the promise of actual things' is about as sound a metaphor for self-study and the resulting institutional strategy as we can offer.

2

SELF-STUDY IN HIGHER EDUCATION

This book is about the use of evidence in the management of universities and colleges. Of course, all managers – of every kind of enterprise – claim to use evidence. In higher education this claim is probably further away from the truth than in most cases. This chapter attempts to establish the state of the art.

We argued in Chapter 1 that self-study is about reflective collective practice – to improve institutional understanding, to support strategic goals and to improve competitive positioning. We also argued that university self-study matters, and matters increasingly given the context in which higher education is now operating. It is likely to underpin institutional health and overall effectiveness in an increasingly competitive environment. It follows that thinking hard about self-study should form part of the university's thinking about strategy and risk as a whole. This implies the need to approach self-study coherently and to manage it robustly, without making it merely a technical adjunct or sacrificing a culture of reflection.

In this chapter, we argue that understanding self-study and how to do it well requires a university to:

- understand the context in which it is doing self-study;
- appraise what it is already doing;
- review that in the light of what others are doing, and of relevant literature about 'good' or 'best' practice'; and
- draw conclusions for enhancing its practice.

In terms of the worked examples given throughout the book, we argue that beginning from the experience of a single institution has explanatory power: it provides a consistent context; it has to 'join up' (and live the consequences of poor fit between) different parts of the activity; and it is true (or at least as true as we can make it).

Injunctions like these apply to any university in reasonable control of its own destiny anywhere in the world. In this book the majority of our analysis of the cultural context is at the level of a nation (the United Kingdom), of political and administrative arrangements at the level of the English sector (including the actions of its funding council), and of the resulting actions of individual institutions in terms of one university (the University of Brighton), which can none the less claim to represent characteristic developmental dilemmas of what the Chancellor of the Exchequer calls 'broadly-based leading universities' (HMT 2004: 6). Climbing back up this tree, we have, however, tried where appropriate to identify the following: what is distinctive about (and distinctively difficult for) Brighton; where there are divergences between English policy and practice and that in the other countries of the UK; and where there are significant lessons to be learned from other parts of the world (in Chapter 7 we return to the large question of the contribution of British higher education to a global community).

Seeking out and then responding to evidence is vital at all of these levels. Ironically, it's not as if higher education institutions (HEIs) lack evidence. Some would say that they are drowning in it.

There is a plethora of evidence produced for external agencies: to justify funding, to reassure stakeholders, or to support bids. In the UK those using such evidence about performance range from funders (the Higher Education Funding Councils [HEFCs], the Teacher Training Agency [TTA] and other government departments like the Department of Health [DoH], as well as the Higher Education Statistics Agency [HESA]), through quality controllers (including the Quality Assurance Agency for Higher Education [QAA] and the Office for Standards in Education [Ofsted]) to statutory bodies (like the Commission for Racial Equality [CRE]).

Meanwhile the life cycle of the educational process itself generates its own waves of information: on recruiting and enrolling students; monitoring their progress through assessment and examination; making awards; tracking alumni destinations; ensuring the viability of research and 'third-leg' activity; other fund-raising; and the like.

We have attempted to capture both the shape and the flavour of these processes by reference to the three overlapping 'cycles' which structure Part 2 of the book: data; quality; and planning.

Arguably, the higher education sector is data-rich – the Higher Education Statistics Agency (HESA) holds over three billion items of data (HESA 2003). Equally arguably, it is intelligence-poor.

Universities invest massively in the people, hardware and software to collect, store and sort the data required by themselves and by external agencies. But there is a general feeling of frustration. A 2003 survey into the use of management information in promoting and achieving strategic focus (based on interviews with representatives of 34 institutions) found that:

- 'the overwhelming majority of respondents believed that their management information only covered some of their strategic objectives ... [they] relied upon more ad hoc methods' (RSM Robson Rhodes 2003: 1);
- 'nearly one third of the respondents thought that their institution was poorly served by its management information. Only three respondents were wholly satisfied' (RSM Robson Rhodes 2003: 1);
- there was particular dissatisfaction about the capacity to use management information to look forward. Other complaints covered data sufficiency, reliability, and comprehensibility. Financial data were most usually regarded as satisfactory (RSM Robson Rhodes (2003: 1 and 16). Half the respondents accepted that staff keep their own records, apart from the institutional systems, and nearly 40 per cent thought that producing useful information from their systems was extremely effortful (RSM Robson Rhodes 2003: 18 and 9).

The first round of institutional audits by the UK's Quality Assurance Agency (QAA) has also identified variability in the quality of institutional management information systems (MIS), some flagging up weaknesses to be addressed. The QAA's overview based on eight of the first audits under the new framework notes that there are 'recommendations for further consideration' in relation to 'the use of management information, particularly statistical data' to inform decision-making and the oversight of quality and standards (QAA 2003a: 1). Similarly, in Wales, early subject engagements 'found that HEIs need to improve the quality and breadth of the statistical information on students, and to enable both subject staff and the institutional administrative staff to share and use the information more effectively' (QAA 2002a).

The national agencies publish copious and often highly detailed reports using the data supplied to them. They put effort into working with colleagues from the sector to improve the technical quality of the data and the clarity of the guidance about its structure and definitions. But the effort that is put into seriously analysing these data and making use of them in self-study – to understand the individual university or the broader sector and to inform decision-making – tends to be scanty in comparison. In addition, it is still too often the case that policy is made in the absence of – or even in the face of – data-based evidence.

There are some important exceptions, when data are published about the sector with a salience and power to convince that forces institutions and funders to sit up and take notice. An example is the longitudinal data published by the Longer Term Strategy Group of Universities UK (UUK) on student demand for subjects and the pattern of provision (see Chapter 4). However, it remains more usual that the data either do not exist or actually need to be ignored in pursuit of policy. For example, as Aston has pointed out, the decision to promote foundation degrees in England is not based on evidence of demand for such a qualification and, indeed, the research available suggests strongly 'honours degrees and sub degrees are two distinct products that are imperfectly substitutable – especially when offered at different types of institution' (HEPI 2003: 8). Much of any additional demand is likely to be for the current honours degree. Similarly, the current preoccupation with improving access to higher education for young adults from low participation neighbourhoods, while necessary, is in danger of ignoring not only how far the UK higher education sector has travelled against a broader definition of widening participation, but also the needs and aspirations of other populations. For example, international comparisons show that the UK student population is considerably more open to older and part-time students, as well as those with disabilities, than much of the rest of Europe (Ramsden 2003: 3–19).

Finally, it is rare for UK institutions to be able to use data to make systematic comparisons with others. In part, as Jackson notes, this is a consequence of the fact that 'the UK higher education system celebrates diversity but the drawback of this approach, compounded by the increasingly competitive nature of the market, means that there are few national bench-marks or opportunities that would enable comparisons of practice and performance to be made' (Jackson 1997: 78). This might explain why Shattock depends so heavily on the rankings offered by the league tables to identify his 'successful universities' despite their fundamental flaws for such a purpose (Shattock 2003a: 1–23).

There *is* a general commitment to improve the current situation. The survey noted above, for example, found that almost all the respondents had projects underway to improve their management information systems, and a number of the QAA institutional audit reports published to date note that institutions are working hard on addressing acknowledged weaknesses in processes and capacities.

The RSM Robson Rhodes survey cited above, for example, found that almost all the respondents had projects underway to improve their management information systems. The Scottish Funding Councils' (SFCFHE) joint corporate plan includes creating a baseline report on higher education in Scotland, to include international comparisons, because 'an important principle underpinning our work is that our policy decisions should draw on the best available evidence' (SFCFHE 2003: 8). This is in the broader UK context of an apparent commitment to improve the extent of evidence-based policy-making and practice, including the creation of an Economic and Social Research Council (ESRC)-funded centre (the Centre for Evidence Based Policy and Practice) (EBPP); the work of the Learning and Teaching Support Network Generic Centre (LTSN) to provoke debate about evidence-based practice in higher education, and a major thrust by the government to increase the salience of social science data and research in government.

But we would agree with informed US commentators who, notwithstanding the more highly developed role for institutional research apparent there (described in more detail below), have raised concerns about the adequacy of efforts. One recent commentary notes that 'too many of the maps and navigation instruments that were once effective guides are now obsolete' and has called for 'the development of a culture of evidence – an environment characterized by a willingness not only to create measures and collect data on outcomes, but also to use this information to redesign practices for improving quality' (Gumport *et al.* 2002: 3 and 6).

Organizational learning and the university

Bringing the analysis in Chapter 1 into the world of higher education, the literature about organizational learning and decision-making appears to offer five lessons for the university.

First, we must eschew assumptions that institutions are rational and take strategic decisions based on perfect information (Whittington 1993; Mintzberg 2000). The rational model requires an environmental predictability and an information-processing capacity that simply do not exist (Whittington 1993) – and assumes both 'perfect knowledge' and 'perfect rationality' (Rosenfield and Wilson 1999: 183–4). It is a fallacy to think that 'the strategy making process is driven by "hard data", comprising quantitative aggregates of the detailed "facts" about the organization and its environment' (Mintzberg 2000: 223–4). In part this is simply because 'strategy making is an immensely complex process involving the most sophisticated, subtle, and at times subconscious of human cognitive and social processes' (Mintzberg 2000: 227). But it is also because the hard data beloved by some writers on planning have a 'soft underbelly' (Mintzberg 2000: 257) and because 'something is always lost in the process of quantification' (Mintzberg 2000: 265). Instead, as discussed in Chapter 1, we should recognize Choo's 'residual equivocality', and that 'there must be something more to strategic choice than just plugging in the techniques' (Whittington 1993: 78; Choo 1998: 260).

Secondly, and despite these reservations, decision-making *can* be improved: through robust heuristics; through better understanding of what is really going on in decision-making in the realms of 'conformity, culture and power' (Rosenfield and Wilson 1999: 184); through ways of facilitating challenge to orthodoxy; through better alignment between the institution and its environment (Watson 2000); or through shifting institutional research from a concentration on technical to contextual intelligence (Chan 1993).

Thirdly, it follows that effective strategy-making will combine the analytic with the intuitive. 'Some issues depend on models locked deep inside the intuitive brains of managers, but other issues are better handled by models that have ... been made formally consistent' (Mintzberg 2000: 330). This is intimately linked to sense-making; helping organizations deal with information overload and ambiguity. This will be based on knowing the organization well, but also on formal analysis assisted by effective systems for managing information. The latter need is probably growing, but solutions do not lie simply in the technology: 'the process of managing data with a view to transforming it into information is a complex strategic one, which should be informed by an understanding of the way in which the organisation itself works' (Milner 2000: 7).

Fourthly, performance measurement plays a problematic part in all this. Some very successful corporations have run for a number of years on the basis of a clear understanding of 'the numbers' (see Whittington 1993, on General Electric). Despite rejecting notions of rationality and perfect information, commentators agree on the need to identify key information of strategic importance. Higher Education (HE) offers models too, whether prescriptive or descriptive, of systems to align key aspects of delivery (Sizer 1989; Shattock 2003a). Measuring the performance of 'their' higher education institutions is a problem vexing governments all around the world as they seek to enlist them in crusades for economic competitiveness or social cohesion.

Finally, recent emphasis on risk management in decision-making and corporate governance underlines the importance of the ability to anticipate and recognize warning signals; to understand relative strengths and weaknesses; to assess the degree, likelihood and impact of each major risk identified; and to manage risks accordingly. This can apply to any area of organizational activity. Appetite for risk will differ across the range of activities (HEFCE 2001a). In HE, it is also possible that a risk-based approach to quality management will emerge. In turn, this implies excellent institutional intelligence and discrimination, as well as having sufficiently effective systems to underpin judgements about risks and their management. The required system of internal control, according to the Turnbull report, 'should be embedded in the operation of the organisation and form part of its culture' (quoted in HEFCE 2001a: 32).

To summarize brutally, universities and colleges can still fall prey to at least two classic dilemmas. The first is the 'Ehrenberg trap', after the Cornell economist Ronald Ehrenberg who, when he was provost of his university, found his colleagues engaged in commissioning and then ignoring vast amounts of data. His maxim is 'if information is not going to be used, don't incur the costs of collecting it' (Ehrenberg 1999). (We should also be wary of the reciprocal of this trap: the excuse for doing nothing that arises from the phrase 'more research needed'.)

The second dilemma is more subtle. There is a vitally important qualitative element in the processes we are attempting to describe, which can, without care, be relegated beneath the pseudo-scientism of management by spreadsheet. Economists know this trap as a variant on Goodhart's law, in its popular form: 'when a measure becomes a target, it ceases to be a good measure' (Watson 2000: 79).

Self-study in higher education: an international perspective

Writing in 2003 in a twenty-fifth anniversary volume for the European Association for Institutional Research (EAIR), Guy Neave reflects that 'it is very far from coincidental that the roots of institutional research lie not in Europe so much as in the United States and, to a lesser extent, the United Kingdom'. His thesis is that the positive influence on its development was not so much 'massification' as the structural fact that US institutions had to take responsibility for 'functions that in Europe were located at central government level and under ministerial oversight, initiative and responsibility' (Neave 2003: 4). This is a plausible explanation for how and why institutions come to take responsibility for 'internal intelligence gathering': it happens when it affects the bottom line, in terms of both reputation and economics.

Certainly the United States leads the world in terms of both the philosophy and practicalities of what we try to describe here. North

American self-study is at the heart of the institutional accreditation process. It probably also leads the world in examples of funding arrangements at state and sometimes institutional level that are predicated on what we might regard as somewhat simplistic incentive models and quantifications of activity (see for example Lombardi 2000).

The American Association for Institutional Research (AIR) celebrated its quarter century in 1985. It has over 3000 members in over 1500 institutions and offers a range of services and publications to members including an ambitious annual forum, research grants and fellowships, a journal and two series of professional support documentation. The approach is unashamedly quantitative, with articles on the merits and examples of applications of particular statistical techniques, but also on the evolving place and profession of institutional research, and sometimes on the politics too. It sets a suitably high-minded ambition for the role of the institutional researcher: 'the systematic appraisal of the higher education effort ... The institutional researcher serves higher education and, in turn, his/her institution, through critical appraisal and careful investigation of its processes and programmes' (Suslow 1971). AIR has also worked hard to help institutions make sensible assessments of quality, to debunk some of the cruder attempts at this and, with others, to expose the flaws in some of the US league tables (see Borden and Owens [2001] and Pike [2004] on ways of assessing quality assessments and the US league tables). Accessible examples of US institutional self-study include Indiana University/Purdue University Indianapolis and the University of Florida. Alongside these are wider programmes including the University of Delaware-led National Study of Instructional Costs and Productivity and the Lombardi Program based at the University of Florida (see list of websites). Recent useful overviews include Knight (2003), Howard (2001) and Volkwein (1999). The AIR website has extensive coverage on particular issues and techniques.

But the rest of the world has been catching up, not just through the genteel and voluntaristic ethos of EAIR, but also as the situation of universities in Australasia, in Continental Europe, in Japan and in the UK has demanded it. Yorke, like Neave, suggests that the critical motive is competitiveness and relative positioning (Yorke 2004: 149–50). The European University Association's (EUA) institution evaluation programme rests on self-evaluation. It identifies the main factors impelling universities to take part in its programme as the specific European tensions between the Lisbon and Bologna agreements – concentration of research funds on the one hand and common quality standards on the other. However, to date it seems to appeal mainly to institutions in countries other than the UK (EUA 2004).

In the UK in 1997, the National Committee of Inquiry into Higher

Education (NCIHE) made a number of recommendations based on the perception that higher education institutions needed to strengthen their capacity for and practice of evaluating or measuring their effectiveness – 'self-study'. These recommendations included the development of a set of sector-wide performance indicators (PIs) and the use of benchmarks; and that each governing body should review 'at least once every five years ... its own effectiveness ... [and] all major aspects of the institution's performance', publishing the results in the university's annual report (NCIHE 1997: recommendation 57).

Arguably, the potential for university self-study has improved considerably since the NCIHE reported in 1997. Much of this has been externally driven and reflects significant technical advances. Examples include:

- the publication by the HEFCE of a suite of performance indicators;
- the 2001 Research Assessment Exercise (RAE), building on the earlier exercises of 1986, 1992 and 1996, and yielding scores for, and in some cases detailed feedback about, the quality of research;
- investment by HEFCE and institutions in work under the Good Management Practice banner;
- completion of the round of subject reviews by the QAA yielding teaching quality scores for much of the sector's provision;
- publication by the TTA of a series of institutional profiles;
- publication by the HESA and the Universities and Colleges Admissions Service (UCAS) of a range of data and management information, increasingly on CD-ROM;
- the general development of analytical techniques drawing on geo-demographics, with newly available information about the characteristics of applicants and entrants, as well as about local populations, enabling both better competitor analysis and attention to policy concerns;
- a plethora of informal information about aspects of performance, notably the various newspaper league tables (which draw largely on published information but combine this in various ways reflecting the political predilections of the publication); and
- promotion by the Learning and Teaching Support Network (LTSN) generic centre (absorbed into the 'Academy') of 'institutional research' including efforts to establish a self-sustaining network for institutional researchers (Jackson 2003).

Nonetheless, these apparent improvements since Dearing mask a number of weaknesses. Much of the information available to assist a university to make judgements about its performance – broadly defined – continues to have substantial limitations, including:

- its currency – with official figures published only some time after their collection;
- its relevance to individual institutions and their objectives;
- its indigestibility by governing bodies, staff, students or potential students and other stakeholders;
- the absence of robust and meaningful comparisons between institutions; and
- the scope for the data and their use to distort university behaviour, largely because of the impact of league tables.

Yet, as we have argued already, the higher education sector is rather poorly placed to achieve the degree of self-knowledge implied by making these sorts of judgements. This reflects largely practical circumstances – for example, there is considerable scepticism about the technical validity of many of the current crop of most frequently used measures of effectiveness. This includes some commonly used performance indicators, where the consensus amongst informed commentators is that intrinsic features of PI, however carefully constructed, include lack of rigour, partiality and distortion of what is being measured (Johnes and Taylor 1990; Yorke 1991; Nedwek and Neal 1994; Cave *et al.* 1997). But it also reflects political reality – the capacity of universities to draw hard conclusions, whether published or not, about their effectiveness and progress must be questioned given the current competitive – and often defensive – climate.

Self-study in practice

This section offers an account of the desirable features of self-study practice if it is to achieve the purposes set out in Chapter 1. It does so by reference to current practice in the US and in the UK. Drawing on exchanges with colleagues at Brighton and elsewhere, as well as the analysis that informs the creation of the new institutional research network (described above), it then offers two ways in which a university might assess its own self-study capacity. It concludes with an account of some of the tensions to be managed if the desirable features are to be achieved.

Our account of self-study in the previous chapter, and of US and UK current practice in this chapter, suggests that self-study has a number of desirable features. In essence, these are that self-study:

- should be a habitual part of institutional management with 'ownership' through both the academic and the executive functions of the institution;

- should focus on reflection and learning;
- is a 'bottom-up' activity and is truly 'collective' – engaging a high proportion of staff as well as students;
- depends on sensible tools, intelligently used;
- needs clear roles and responsibilities;
- must reflect institutional character and ambitions;
- needs to have as its primary goal understanding and enhancing student learning and the quality of the student experience but to embrace research and 'third stream' activity too;
- must be kept in proportion; and
- must be sustained.

This book takes self-study to be highly practical activity, even if it takes place in a complex theoretical as well as political context. In thinking critically about the sector's and our own university's practice, we do not suggest that the University of Brighton has got everything right. We have chosen to treat self-study as an operation to be managed and therefore to subject the university's practice to the sorts of tests commonly used to assess and improve operations management (Slack *et al.* 2001). Exchanges with colleagues in other institutions chime well with our own identified common concerns about the content and process of self-study as currently practised, as summarized below.

- This work is necessarily growing, but is still hampered by difficulties in defining and gathering useful information that is current and valid for all areas of activity.
- Boards of Governors (and their equivalent) are exerting pressure to develop and/or use a comprehensive set of indicators of performance or progress. While these may be linked to the HEFCE PIs, many also want to ensure that they will be directly related to the university's own aspirations. In turn, this reflects the growing recognition that understanding effectiveness needs to be linked to institutional planning and decision-making – the achievement of objectives, comparing and contrasting the position of schools or departments within the institution as well as institutional-level comparisons: how to demonstrate whether or not the university is, in the words of one of our respondents, 'in good shape'.
- Universities are concerned about the resource implications of doing a better job of self-study, recognizing that increased effort must still be manageable and must yield results that justify increased investment.
- Effort is often put into testing off-the-shelf packages, including the balanced scorecard and European Framework for Quality

Management (EFQM). However, these are sometimes felt to be both over-elaborate to carry out and over-simplistic in their underlying assumptions. To date, there seems no obvious general move to embrace these in the UK.

- It is increasingly common for one university to compare its performance with that of a selected group of others, and to consider the results at the highest levels of the institution and in key committees. However, this relies on published data and has certain limitations.

- A number of universities are supplementing the HEFCE PIs with indicators developed in-house. Much work is underway to refine understanding. As one of our respondents explained, the institution is looking for 'measures which really do monitor the effectiveness of, and focus on, the...core strategies and in particular, provide some kind of warning light...to indicate when things are not being quite so effective'.

- There is growing concern that more staff throughout institutions should understand their institution's relative position and performance.

- The medium-term ambition is to be able to demonstrate that better self-study is leading to better decision-making. One respondent put this in context: 'certainly in a year or so I would expect to see a clear linkage between the identification of performance measures for improvement (as a direct result of the internal performance analysis) and the development and implementation of new key strategies to address these'.

Conceptualizing self-study as an operation to be managed prompts two ways of thinking about how it can be improved. The first is to examine why the institution's understanding of its own effectiveness is less well developed than it might be. This is about cause and effect: what are the causes of the weaknesses in institutional self-study? Using an operations-management typology, areas of performance can be grouped under the traditional headings of 'people', 'systems', 'materials', and 'resources'. This is illustrated for the University of Brighton in Figure 2.1.

The second way to assess self-study practice (with a view to improving it) is to start with an ideal end-point – to compare what the university wants to achieve with what it is currently able to achieve, on two dimensions: the capacity for self-study; and the fit with its chosen fields of activity (or 'coverage'). This can be achieved by talking with colleagues who both generate and use the information, including Board members (or their equivalent), by assessing a university's practice in discussion with colleagues from other

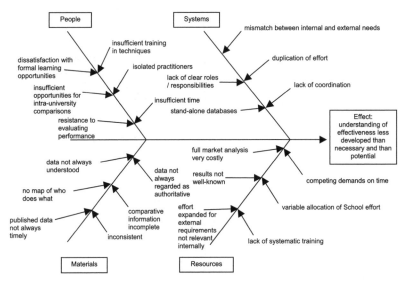

Figure 2.1 Cause/effect of current weaknesses in the practice of self-study

universities, or by comparing it with relevant aspects of the various good practice guides produced by HEFCE. Meanwhile, the institution has to make space to learn from such evidence and to commission further study, ideally upon as broad a base as possible. This entails creating specific 'institutional learning opportunities' such as those which arise from staff development, from study days and seminars, and above all from clear, coherent and accessible internal accounts of the outputs of self-study.

Using these sources, a university might reach some useful conclusions about areas for attention, where the gap between 'actual' and 'desired' performance indicates the amount of work to be done on its self-study processes. Figures 2.2 and 2.3 indicate this approach for the University of Brighton. Figure 2.2 looks at self-study capacity, and suggests that the university is relatively comfortable about certain aspects of its capacity, other than on internal benchmarking and ability to learn; but that some gaps exist about the level of understanding across the institution and in respect of information for the Board of Governors.

Figure 2.3 looks at the coverage of institutional self-study. This suggests that Brighton has more work to do on aspects of costing (especially with the advent of full economic costing [FEC]), on understanding and responding to the market, and on what is possible as opposed to what is being currently achieved.

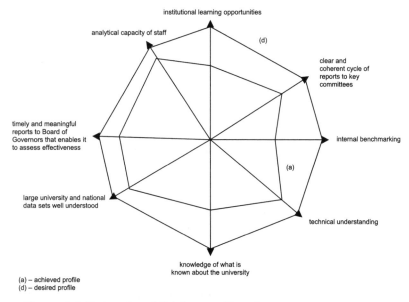

Figure 2.2 University of Brighton: self-study capacity

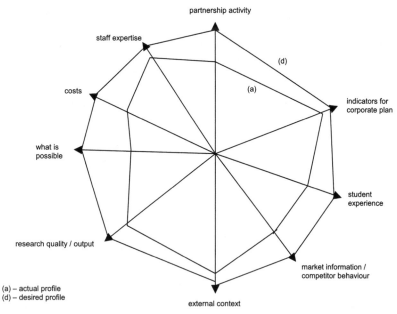

Figure 2.3 University of Brighton: self-study coverage

Above all, it is probably most important to take comfort from the fact that this is a dynamic and evolving field. No institution will achieve comprehensive coverage, or be able to incorporate all of the latest methodological wrinkles, still less to answer all of the legitimate requests for information and advice. As in so many fields, a balance must be struck between modesty and aspiration; between the art of the possible and the drive for continuous improvement.

3

SELF-STUDY: A UNIVERSITY PERSPECTIVE

This book is about how an individual institution goes about what Neave calls 'internal intelligence gathering', and, even more importantly, how it can use the results (Neave 2003). This chapter examines the problems and prospects of the technique as seen from 'inside'.

Purposes

From the perspective of an individual college or university, the purposes of institutional self-study can probably be boiled down to three:

- to understand – and hence to enhance – institutional performance against publicly stated goals;
- to support strategic choices, not least by understanding the environment in which the institution operates; and
- to establish – and strive to improve – the institution's competitive position.

The first is about institutional health (academic and financial); the second is about strategic scoping; and the third is about benchmarking. In all three of these areas there are special considerations which apply to the context, culture and capacity of higher education (as other 'guides' in this series have made clear).

The main goal is both to inform and to validate the institution's Corporate Plan. This incorporates a set of indicators of success – some qualitative, mostly quantitative, against which progress can be measured, as set out in Table 3.1.

Table 3.1 University of Brighton *Corporate Plan 2002–07*: aims and indicators of success

Aim	*Indicators of success*
1 The University will continue to sustain an extensive, challenging and high quality academic portfolio by combining assured standards with flexibility of response.	• Expanded its provision in order to meet the needs of some additional 1500 undergraduates, 700 additional postgraduates and 150 international students; • Completed a further institutional audit resulting in the highest level of confidence in its quality assurance processes; • Completed 18 internal subject reviews; • Completed 6 institutional audits of partner colleges which furnish adequate levels of confidence; and • Sustained its involvement in quality assurance on behalf of the sector by maintaining engagement of staff from each major subject area as external examiners.
2 The University will continue to nurture its intellectual capital ethically, imaginatively and sustainably, and make this widely available.	• 40% of its academic staff conducting research at national or international standards of excellence; • Increased the number of research students by some 100; • Increased research-related income to 15% of total income (by 2010); • Developed a more explicit research leadership role for the University's professoriate and appointed sufficient additional professors to deliver the research strategy; • Increased its income from third stream activities by 7% a year compound growth, in line with its commercial strategy; • Made further annual awards for Innovation; and

Aim	Indicators of success
	• Secured the necessary investment in research space for science and for art and design.
3 The University will continue to equip its students with the skills, knowledge and enthusiasm necessary to learn successfully and to secure employment.	• Sustained its student retention and achievement rates at or above the relevant benchmark; • Sustained its graduate employment rate at or above its benchmark and amongst the highest in the sector; • Increased the number of part-time postgraduate opportunities by at least 400; • Increased by 200 the number of opportunities for students to take part in structured volunteering and ensure that they can have that work recognized within their degrees; • Made further annual awards to recognize excellence in teaching and in supporting students; and • Refined the definition of performance standards for student services.
4 The University will continue to collaborate actively with selected local, regional, national and international partners on the basis of mutual respect.	• Moved closer to its benchmark for the proportion of young entrants from lower social classes and low participation neighbourhoods and sustained its position above the benchmark in respect of their previous education; • Increased the amount of income generated through partnership with EU institutions; • Secured with partners a complete 'qualifications map' for post-16 learners from the locality, including expansion in the number of level 1 and 2 opportunities in partner colleges, and opportunities for progression

Aim	Indicators of success
	to level 3 and beyond at the University; • Played its part in the opening of the Brighton and Sussex Medical School; and • Opened the University Centre Hastings.
5 The University will further improve the environment in which members of its community study, work and live, and will contribute positively to the wider environment.	• Completed phase 3 of the redevelopment of the Falmer campus, including purpose-built accommodation to support the University's role in the Brighton and Sussex Medical School, and made substantial progress towards completing phases 4 and 5; • Secured significant increases in the number of student residences provided on its behalf in Brighton and Eastbourne; • Made substantial progress towards the redevelopment of library provision for the Grand Parade site; • Created and opened for business an innovation centre on the Moulescoomb site; • Achieved hospitality assured accreditation for catering and conference services; • Sustained progress in securing lower environmental impact in managing its estate and facilities; and • Established student use of the VLE in 75% of undergraduate modules by (July 2005).
6 The University will continue to manage and govern itself with responsibility and sensitivity.	• Secured the objectives in the staffing strategy (2001–04) and agreed further development plans to ensure that the progress achieved can be sustained; • Maintained general reserves at

Aim	Indicators of success
	least meeting the HEFCE-recommended level of 3% of turnover;
	• Maintained an investment fund of £10m;
	• Maintained a Foundation Fund of £1m; and
	• Developed indicators of performance and effectiveness that better underpin planning and decision making.

Source: Appendix 1 (2003a)

We return to the question of achievement against these goals in Chapter 6.

Components

Self-study at the University of Brighton has the following components.

Three annual information cycles involving the systematic collection and scrutiny of information about the university. These are the data cycle, the quality cycle and the planning cycle. A trio of large – and growing – data sets underpins them, handling student data (enrolments, characteristics, and academic progress); finance; and staffing.

The **data cycle** focuses on collecting and analysing data on student applications, enrolments and retention, graduate destinations, student characteristics and key financial indicators. Analyses are considered – in different levels of aggregation – from School to Board level. A time series is underway. Comparisons are made routinely between targets and achievements. External reporting is a strong feature. Several of the data sets and collection processes are subject to external audit. Within the data cycle, there is a sub-cycle based on **surveys** and data analysis, with the results reported through the main committee structure. This includes an annual survey of student finances, students' reasons for choosing Brighton or for declining their offer, staff sickness data, student characteristics, and reasons for leaving the university (Appendix 1 2001a, 2001b, 2002b, 2003d, 2003e, 2003g). In several cases (notably student finance), these have built up powerful longitudinal data sets that can be used to evaluate and influence national policy. A second sub-cycle is based on

performance indicators, comprising regular reports to the Board of Governors drawing on published PIs and comparing the university's performance with that of a group of comparator universities. A third essential sub-cycle is the monthly **Management Information Report** (MIR) presenting the data about aspects of the university's financial position including actual against expected income and expenditure; the stock and flow of research grant income; and cash and debtor balances. The full MIR is received by the university's Management Group and a summary is also received at Board level, by the Finance and Employment Committee (Appendix 1 2004i).

At the heart of the data cycle is the **Annual Academic Year Review**. This is a comprehensive survey of university performance, underpinned by support departments' accounts of their work during the previous year. Presented to the first meeting of the Academic Board in the session, it provides an essential context for self-evaluation and for future planning at all levels of the organization.

The **quality cycle** is founded on a mass of effort at School level to analyse data primarily on student performance and on the quality of the student experience. This is directed at supporting individual students, enhancing the quality of their academic and social experience, assessing the effectiveness of teaching and learning as well as the infrastructure which underlies it, checking on the relevance and currency of the curriculum, and discharging external quality assurance requirements including the response to external examiners' reports. It includes stopping to think, especially when things go wrong and students complain (Appendix 1 2003m).

At the heart of the quality cycle lies the **Annual Academic Health Process** and the resulting **Report**, usually presented to the Academic Board meeting in March each session. This is essentially a retrospective analysis of the strengths and weaknesses of the university's work over the preceding year, together with a review of activity against a particular theme (such as student retention or student feedback). The Process is based on hard data, and includes an 'enhancement day' at which priorities for action are agreed and progress against the previous year's practice is assessed.

The **planning cycle** involves setting objectives and assessing progress towards them, reflecting on findings from the quality and data cycles, and responding to external drivers. It takes place at levels from individual School/department to the Board of Governors.

At the heart of the planning cycle is the university **Annual Report**, published with the financial accounts for the previous year. This is structured around progress against the institution's broader corporate objectives and represents a top-level view from the Board of Governors. It also provides a context for the reports required by the funding council (HEFCE), which include both five-year financial forecasts and an annual monitoring statement, which, in the Brighton version, includes some thirty university-wide targets. HEFCE also requires a critical appraisal of work in specified areas (such as widening participation, learning and teaching, human resource management and 'third stream' activity) where it is providing earmarked or formula-driven funds.

The quality, planning and data cycles are discussed in greater length in the next three chapters. Vital issues relating to **financial self-study** have been embedded in these and subsequent chapters rather than separately highlighted. These are covered more explicitly in another volume in this series (Thomas 2001: see especially pp. 108–39). Since Thomas's book appeared there have been additional external drivers here which we reflect in what follows. These include:

- the government-instigated 'transparency review' (TRAC);
- the funding councils' value for money (VFM) initiatives (including studies of managing energy, treasury, building repairs and maintenance; Information Systems; facilities; and student administration);
- company and charity legislation;
- sector guidance on risk management; and
- the sector's move towards financial 'listing', through the work of agencies like Standard and Poor's.

In addition to these 'hard' cycles, there are some 'softer' approaches at work too. These include the university's **organizational learning cycle**, comprising:

- a set of five annual conferences open to all staff – on widening participation; learning and teaching; learning technologies; higher education research; and student retention;
- the Management Forum – termly meetings of the university's most senior forty or so staff;
- the Senior Staff Seminar – termly meetings of the same group with a developmental focus;
- termly Board of Governors seminars.

There is, finally, an **ongoing review of governance effectiveness**. Instituted in 1999 following the Dearing Report, the first iteration made a number of recommendations, including about the need to establish a set of indicators of performance at Board level that would enable comparative judgements to be made with other universities. It has been followed up in 2004 with a review of the ways in which the Board is able to assess the university's own progress (Appendix 1 2004e).

Ad hoc reviews and data analysis also go on, often in response to issues emerging from one of the cycles described above or in response to requests from individual Schools. Some of these are 'one-off' or periodic like the following:

- analysis of data on staff sickness absence (Appendix 1 2001a);
- a questionnaire on work/life balance for staff (Appendix 1: Cooper 2001);
- a review of provision for part-time students through a survey and focus groups (Appendix 1: Webb 1998);
- a survey of alumni (Appendix 1 2003f); and
- a consumer survey of catering services (Appendix 1 2003l) and regular surveys of library users (Appendix 1 2004h).

Alongside this, academic and professional staff research aspects of HE policy and practice based on their experience at Brighton that can also support options appraisal, decision-making, and the enhancement of practice. Recent examples include:

- work on the newly emerging professional doctorate (Bourner *et al.* 2000);
- a survey of 'studentification' (the concentration and impact of students in private sector residential accommodation in Brighton and Eastbourne) (Appendix 1 2003k);
- a survey of the experience of newly appointed lecturers (Appendix 1 2003h);
- investigation of student characteristics and widening participation strategies and their effectiveness (Appendix 1 2001b);
- reflection on lessons learned from student retention projects (Appendix 1 2003i); and
- reflection on ways of supporting the development of IT skills for learning and teaching (Haynes *et al.* 2004).

While not always focusing solely on the Brighton experience, these pieces of research tend to include it in their scope. In addition, a number of staff carry out work on aspects of university performance as part of their formal studies rather than their jobs (typically, dissertations for the university's MBA or other taught Masters and Doctorates).

Roles and responsibilities ■

This all suggests a mass of effort and also – as set out in Chapter 6 – a real role in institutional planning and decision-making. The effort is directly related to the roles and responsibilities of the university's Board of Governors and committee structure, as well as to the set of indicators of success specified in the Corporate Plan (Appendix 1 2003a). The resulting set of relationships is illustrated in Figure 3.1.

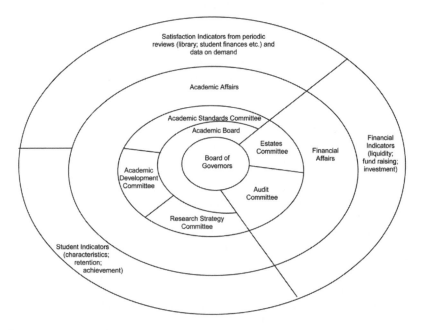

Figure 3.1 Self-study at the University of Brighton: roles and responsibilities

At the heart of all of these issues is the hoary old question of 'ownership' across the institution. We are aware of how brittle this concept can be as a call to arms in a professionally argumentative and intellectually diverse community like a university or college. A subsidiary theme is therefore the ways in which different parts of the community – subject-based academics and professionally orientated support staff – can be encouraged to see embedding self-study as integral to the achievement of their own goals.

PART 2 SELF-STUDY IN ACTION

4

THE DATA CYCLE

This book is about how universities can systematically ensure that they have the information they need to take wise and transparent decisions. This chapter is about how they can turn relevant, high-quality data into valuable information, through designing and operating an effective data cycle.

Information is, after all, 'the sustenance of university life ... Collecting, organizing, analysing and disseminating information is essential for good management and decision-making' (O'Donovan 2000: 65). The successful university needs high-quality data to aid high-quality and open decision-making: 'not only will good data stimulate performance in departments but it strengthens the institution's grip on strategy' (Shattock 2003a: 95). It is also vital in order to avoid crises: 'institutions should provide themselves with state-of-the-art management information systems, so that senior managers cannot remain under any illusions about the true state of their "business" and must become "data-rich institutions" to avoid the fate of those that have experienced highly publicised crises over the last twenty or so years' (Scott 2003: 174 and 176).

The first of the three big cycles to be explored in this book is therefore the data cycle.

The data framework

We noted in Chapter 1 the importance of signals (and of heeding them) for organizational learning and, in Chapter 2, some of the frustrations about the current use and availability of information in higher education, and evidence of perceived systems limitations. We also noted the fallacy of thinking that the answer to big institutional issues lies in collecting more and more data, or in over-simplified performance measurement.

In this chapter, we identify some of the ways in which one university, Brighton, is trying to bring some order to the mass of data and way it is organized and made available. The purpose of our data cycle is to provide intelligent answers to questions about performance, broadly defined, in a timely, robust and manageable way. This should inform strategic and operational decisions and should support reflection about the impact of previous decisions.

There are two main audiences, each of which has different but overlapping data requirements: the institution itself, and external bodies. In addition to these, there are also the increasingly important audiences of the media and, more than ever, students and their families and other advisers.

The totality of the data involved in the data framework is played out in a set of data collections and analyses. This is illustrated in Table 4.1, indicating the date, content and internal and external audience.

The resulting data framework is a complicated beast, with:

- a mixture of activities and frequency;
- highly distributed consideration of the data and conclusions to be drawn, by many different parts of the university's committee and decision-making apparatus;
- a high volume of external requirements, with varying relevance to internal requirements, each of which can be subject to audit – but also a wealth of internal activity that is not determined by external requirements;
- varying methodologies, ranging from surveys of individual students to desktop research using published data;
- varying uses, ranging from internal resource allocation and planning decisions to a broader informing of policy and practice;
- a strong relationship to university planning, to monitoring progress against plans, and to aspects of quality, with the data cycle therefore underpinning the planning and quality cycles; and
- the capacity to look at comparisons over time, but, in contrast, relatively little attention to comparisons between institutions.

This account indicates the considerable variety in the type of data for self-study adopted by the University, including: annual surveys of student perception and finances; what have become routine analyses of data from the larger institutional data systems; and one-off reviews

Table 4.1 University of Brighton: data framework

Date	Content	Use – internal/considered by	Use – external
Autumn	Student enrolments – 1 December census date	Counts students by price group (underpinned by a more detailed breakdown). Informs decisions on resource allocations and future size and shape of institution Management Group; Academic Development Committee; Academic Board; Board of Governors	HESES Drives decisions about compliance with the HEFCE contract
September	Staff activity	Counts number of staff by subject Not used internally	HESA Included in data for some league tables
October	Initial Teacher Training enrolments – 15 October census date	Individual count of students enrolled on TTA-funded courses Faculty Management Group	TTA Drives decisions about TA contract compliance
Autumn	Analysis of student academic appeals	Summary report of issues and outcomes, distribution across the university. Can suggest areas of concern Academic Board	
Winter	Reasons for students to choose or reject the university	Survey of enrolled students and those who reject offers: 'softer' contribution to decisions about portfolio and processes Recruitment Group, Management Group	
Winter	Student financial circumstances	Survey of enrolled students. Provides information about perceived pressures, needs for support services, and changes in circumstances between groups and over time	Published report

Date	Content	Use – internal/considered by	Use – external
		Academic Board, Board of Governors	
December	Research activity – students, staff, contracts	Measures volumes of activity. Used to assess progress against corporate plan and Faculty strategic plans; helps plan for future research developments Research Strategy Committee	Research Activity Survey
January	Annual report	Critically assesses progress across the range of activity especially against the Corporate Plan indicators of success Audit Committee and Board of Governors	Published report and accounts, for general accountability
January	PIs analysis	Analyses HEFCE PIs. Used to highlight areas of change and progress relative to corporate plan objectives Academic Development Committee; Board of Governors	Media
February	Student retention report	Analyses student retention by School Student Retention Review Group; Academic Standards Committee; Faculty Management Groups	Separate calculation of retention within funding council PIs
By July	Key operating targets	Assesses achievement against corporate objectives. Identifies strengths and weaknesses Management Group, Academic Development Committee, Academic Board, Board of Governors	University Annual Report; HEFCE annual monitoring statement

Date	Content	Use – internal/considered by	Use – external
Summer	Student achievement data	Data on assessment outcomes School Boards, Faculty Academic Boards	
Summer	External examiner reports	Analysis of reports Pro-Vice-Chancellor and Vice-Chancellor, with Deans	
Monthly	Management Information Report	Assesses key financial indicators including expenditure against budget, research grants awarded. Offers early warning of financial difficulties (e.g. levels of student debt) Management Group; summary to Finance and Employment Committee (Board of Governors)	
Monthly	Released vacancies	Lists staff movements and posts to be filled. Enables management of vacancies, and thus of cash/commitments, and matching staff resource to planned activity Management Group	
Monthly	NHS enrolments	Measures volume of nursing and PAMS education delivered including retention rates Faculty Management Group	Drives decisions about NHS contract compliance
Monthly	Applications data, cumulative applications tracker (plus annual sector trends analysis)	Identifies trends in demand and likely achievement against recruitment targets. Enables corrective action to targets for current year and informs decisions about new course developments and future planning	

Date	Content	Use – internal/considered by	Use – external
		Admissions Forum, Management Group, Academic Development Committee, Recruitment Group, Board of Governors (summary)	
Five times a year	Indicators of performance	Assesses relative achievement and delivery, comparative data. Identifies similarities and differences between the university and others, and between the university and its corporate plan indicators of success; prompts questions Board of Governors	
Ongoing	Questionnaire to non-completing students	Summary of responses, can identify areas of general or specific concern Student Retention Review Group and Academic Standards Committee	
Ongoing	Analysis of costs, plus Transparency Review	Regular analysis of costs of new and ongoing activities Faculty Management Groups; support Departments; Management Group on particular issues	TRAC

on particular topics. There is also useful work done by individual University staff who choose to reflect critically on aspects of provision and to share their findings, not included in the table. These range across a number of dimensions, from the simple or descriptive to the analytic or complex and from the qualitative to the quantitative. The resulting variety of self-study data is illustrated in Figure 4.1.

There are perhaps three important points to make about this representation. First, there are some interesting omissions. The

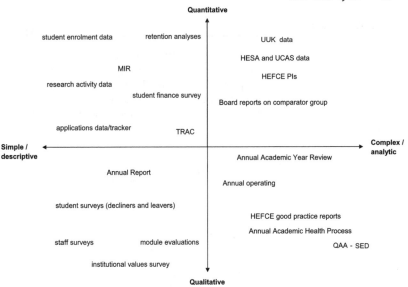

Figure 4.1 Varieties of data for self-study

University has, for example, not been persuaded by the work of Lee Harvey and others who put much of their quality data effort into institution-wide surveys of student opinion and who lean towards student satisfaction as a proxy for quality (Geal *et al.* 1997). It does, of course, commission student feedback on modules and courses and will be developing models that reflect emerging guidance on student feedback at the institutional level, and will have to play its full part in the National Student Survey (NSS). Nor does it have survey-based data about the way its staff use their time within an overall workload, apart from the limited form of the early Transparency Review (TRAC) methodology (although it does have a model – based on the teaching staff contract – for agreeing how time should be used). Secondly, the range of techniques is suggestive of a serious attempt to capture the inherent complexity of the institution's activities – a further illustration of the plethora of evidence, as well as an indication that 'single issue' – or indeed 'single method' – data analysis will rarely be useful. Thirdly, this representation substantiates the need for an effective data cycle to reflect the understanding that 'the process of managing data with a view to transforming it into information is a complex strategic one, which should be informed by an understanding of the way in which the organisation itself works' (Milner 2000: 7).

The data cycle

To make this framework dynamic, the information collected needs to flow around the institution to provide effective support to decision-making and to support the planning and quality cycles. The data are useless if not shared or if not applied to real and challenging questions of policy and performance. This is illustrated schematically in Figure 4.2.

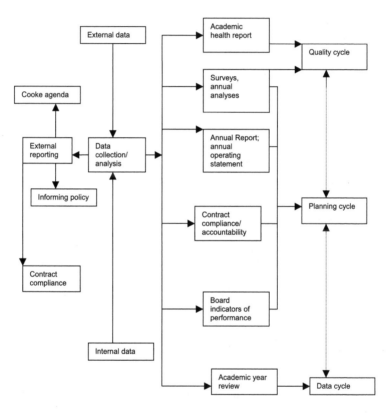

Figure 4.2 Data flows

An effective data cycle will share some of the characteristics of the planning and quality cycles, in that it will be:

- strongly integrated with other institutional activity, particularly the planning and quality cycles, and the committee or business cycle, with certain of its outputs considered by the Board of Governors or Council, and with clearly defined roles and responsibilities;

- focused on the institution's own objectives and grounded in its own practices;
- well organized and managed, to meet internal and external requirements;
- focused on the key dimensions of performance identified by the institution and on delivering appropriate ways of assessing and reporting on performance against stated objectives; and
- supportive of risk management.

In addition, it needs to be:

- realistic about how university performance can be evaluated;
- sensitive to circumstances where data may have to be satisfactory rather than perfect, and about the standards of evidence that should be expected;
- attentive both to accurate data collection and to high-quality data analysis;
- capable of generating useful and, wherever possible, challenging information to colleagues across the institution, as well as information (and commentary) for public consumption;
- intelligent in the use it makes of external information; and
- accompanied by engagement in debates about the collection, management, analysis and use of data and information about the institution and the sector.

The University of Brighton's data cycle is illustrated in Figure 4.3.

The student life cycle

At the heart of the data framework and cycle lies the need to understand the effectiveness of the university's interaction with its students. One way of giving some kind of conceptual and practical shape to this mass of data is to use the 'student life cycle' model (articulated by HEFCE to support work on widening participation and retention) or, conceptually preferable, the 'student journey' (HEFCE 2001b). The University's suite of annual surveys and analyses can be mapped onto this as follows:

- **Pre-entry** includes data of two sorts. The first is about outreach activity with partner schools and colleges, and with individual

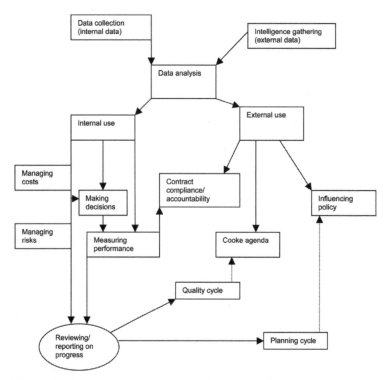

Figure 4.3 University of Brighton: the data cycle

pupils, designed largely to try to widen participation to higher education generally rather than to recruit to Brighton specifically. Much of this work is actually done in partnership with other HEIs under the AimHigher initiative and under the pre-existing Sussex Liaison and Progression Accord. The relationships between such collaborative initiatives and an institution's own data cycle will need careful articulation, and the work will also need to draw on the sorts of external data described below. The second sort of data is about the University's market position amongst potential applicants and we say more about **market intelligence** below.

- **Admission and induction** covers data about **applications** and about **recruitment**. It includes data on the applications cycle, including monitoring of overall volumes and detailed shifts between courses, subjects, Schools and years, as well as the specific tools for tracking and making comparisons described below.
- **Moving through the course** covers data about how students are progressing and, particularly, about their retention. The annual

student retention report offers a statistical analysis at School level of data about student retention and withdrawal. It compares each School with the university and subject benchmark and identifies factors underpinning the data, for example in terms of student characteristics such as gender, age and ethnicity (Appendix 1 2002a, 2002d, 2004c). The data analysis is complemented by a questionnaire to departing students about their reasons for leaving. A case study is supplied in Chapter 9.

• **Achievement, employment and progression** covers data about student outcomes, including assessments at module and course level, routinely considered by Course and Area Boards. We say more about this in Chapter 5. It also includes data on employability and other destinations, including those data largely collected through the arrangements in place under the DLHE (Destinations of Leavers from Higher Education). These data are included in the scope of the **Annual Academic Health Process**, with Heads of School expected to comment on the pattern of destinations of their graduating cohorts, changes between years, variances between courses or subject areas and so on. These data are turned nationally into the employment PIs by the funding councils, which allow some inter-institutional comparisons. There are also some 'softer' data represented in alumni narratives and networking, but this is (at least at Brighton) far from systematic.

External requirements

We have already noted that much of the purpose of the data cycle remains to satisfy external requirements. These requirements are growing as a result of the desire to create better informed 'consumers' of higher education and to meet the accountability requirements of various stakeholders, despite the best intentions of those dedicated to delivering 'better regulation', or a 'lighter touch'. Any management information system therefore needs to be able to meet both the internal and external requirements, preferably without duplication or excessive costs. HESA data collections currently cover five main sets: on students; student first destinations (DLHE); staff; finance; and non-credit-bearing courses. Both HEFCE and HESA data are subject to audit and there are strong penalties for falling foul of the complicated rules for counting and reporting on student numbers in particular. In addition, both the TTA and Department of Health have contract-related data requirements with their own census dates and, in the latter case, monthly returns about students on course. The combined requirements are illustrated in Table 4.2. Note that this representation focuses on compulsory data 'returns'. Alongside this list (not included here) are additional returns required of institutions seeking to unlock various funding streams, or invited, in response to consultations.

We noted in Chapter 2 that HESA, HEFCE, UCAS and the TTA work hard to put the data they collect back into the public domain, often in CD-ROM versions that enable institutions to make their own analyses (for example, the well-regarded Planning Plus series) as well as online services and a series of hard copy volumes from HESA. HESA also offers a bespoke service by which universities can purchase additional data designed to investigate specific questions. However, there can be a time lag between the currency of the data and their publication, although publication on CD-ROM and online is speeding this up. These data provide a valuable resource for universities seeking a better understanding of the sector and their own place within it on a number of measures, as well as to higher education researchers.

There are two contradictory forces at work here. The first is about discharging accountability for funding and is led by the Better Regulation Review Group (BRRG) following up earlier work by the Better Regulation Task Force (BRTF), with 'work aimed at reducing unnecessary bureaucracy, notably with regard to the prospective reduction in data collection requirements on higher education institutions' (BRRG 2003: 3). This reflects the principle 'that regulation must be targeted and proportionate to the problem identified' (BRRG 2003: 4). Problems highlighted by the BRRG include the proliferation of funding streams, often with their own data requirements; a perception by institutions of micromanagement from funding bodies; high transaction costs; and poorly coordinated quality assurance regimes. The BRRG will almost certainly affect the design and operation of institutional data cycles, with consultation on specific data collections, discussions about ways of bringing collections together and enabling data transfer, and wider collaboration between educational data agencies.

The second is largely about creating better informed 'customers' or 'stakeholders' of higher education. The Cooke Report brought together current thinking about the sorts of information that potential students and their advisers might find useful, and resulted in a set of recommendations about publishing sets of data about quality and standards electronically, referred to as Teaching Quality Information (TQI), through the HERO portal (HEFCE 2002b). Indeed, so seriously is the provision of this sort of information being taken by the funders and regulators that institutional progress towards meeting the Cooke requirements on information about quality and standards and the

Table 4.2 External data requirements – annual cycle

Month	Request for information
January	Costs of activities for previous financial year under the TRAC methodology
February	HESA-derived statistics for funding allocation and monitoring
February	HESES-HESA recreate
March	Mid-year financial return
March	Destination of Leavers from Higher Education (DLHE)
Spring	Higher Education–Business Interaction Survey
June	Consultation on performance indicators (draft data)
July	Public supplies, works and services contracts awarded
July	Annual monitoring statement, corporate planning statement and financial forecasts (includes details on staffing, 'third stream', and widening participation activities)
July	TTA skills tests registrations
September	Individual student record
September	New individualized staff record (NISR)
September	Non-credit-bearing aggregate record (NCB)
October	Initial teacher training census data
November	In-service education student numbers return
December	HESA Financial Record
December	Higher Education Students Early Statistics Survey (HESES)
December	Research Activity Survey
December	Update of assignment of departments to academic cost centres
December	Estate management statistics
Annually	Audited financial statements and statement of governance practice
By December 2004 and updated thereafter	Data to be published on the TQI site of the HERO portal including data on entry qualifications, completion, awards, first destinations, summaries of external examiners' reports
Monthly	Contract monitoring (student numbers and movement) for Strategic Health Authority

Note: Shows HEFCE, TTA and DoH data requirements

reliance that can be placed on that information have been included as key considerations of the QAA in its institutional audits.

Despite the efforts by the data agencies and funding bodies to rationalize data requirements, the volume of data, the work required by institutions to generate it, its real utility, and the extent to which this represents intrusion into, or distortion of, institutional management remain matters of concern. There are those who regard the apparent increase in external measurement of performance as part of the growth of the 'evaluative state' (Neave 1998), and antipathetic to the particular nature of higher education, with '[a] realm of hermeneutic transactions (the academy) becoming colonised by a technicism linked to purposive knowledge interests rooted in surveillance, control and external direction' (Barnett 1994: 175). This applies particularly to concerns about performance indicators (PIs). A review of the 'accountability costs' facing institutions by PA Consulting highlights the tensions well. While it notes reductions in the costs of external accountability since its first report, published in 2000, it also notes 'the number of new accountability requirements imposed on HEIs since our first review' from stakeholders including government departments, notably to report on 'third stream' activity; and the concerns of the sample universities about the impact of the proposals for the Office for Fair Access (OFFA), Teaching Quality Information (TQI) and Full Economic Costing (FEC) (PA Consulting 2004b: 2).

Using external data

The intelligent institution will make extensive use of external data about the sector when this is put into the public domain, while recognizing its limitations. The most comprehensive use of the HESA data for analysis is that by Ramsden in the three reports commissioned by the UUK Longer Term Strategy Group, intended as a 'yearbook for higher education' (UUK 2001a, 2002, 2003). These reports aim to correct the tendency that 'too often in the past opinion and instinct have trumped evidence and analysis when assessing performance, policy and practice' (UUK 2001a: 2). The reports offer a sector view derived from the key HESA data sets, concentrating on major trends in student numbers, in the size and shape of the sector, and in financial security. The second and third reports in the series have also taken a specific theme, when updating the base data. The second looks at issues of diversity between institutions – 'the observable but essentially unplanned differences between institutions' (UUK 2002: 2). The third looks at issues of differentiation – 'the conscious identification of many higher education institutions with named groups' (UUK 2003: 2).

By tracking itself against the sector, the institution can place itself against the sector (UK-wide) and the voluntary and other sub-groups within it on a number of dimensions. Figures 4.4 to 4.9 illustrate this on the following dimensions: part-time recruitment; international recruitment; the class base of recruitment; 'public' funding of research; administrative costs; and relative financial security. They show the University of Brighton's position alongside that of major sector groupings (each of which operates on the basis of self-selection) (CMU – Coalition of Mainstream Universities; the 94 Group – pre-1992 universities that aspire to research intensity; Russell Group – research-intensive universities; SCOP – Standing Conference of Principals of HE colleges; non-aligned – institutions that are not members of any of the other groups).

A second major source of external intelligence for any institution are the analytical reports about practice produced, commissioned or stimulated by HEFCE. There are three main types:

- Formal good practice reports. These include guidance on planning and on costing that have implications for the design and operation of the data cycle. However, opinions about the utility, quality and indeed the appropriateness of these are quite varied, partly according to the size and experience of the institution, and its

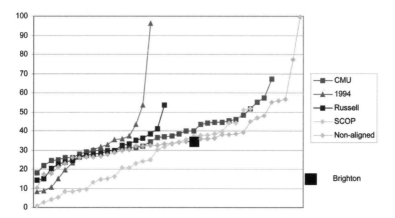

Figure 4.4 UK HE: part-time recruitment
Source: UUK (2003: 21)

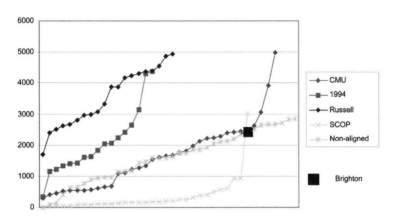

Figure 4.5 UK HE: international recruitment
Source: UUK (2003: 22)

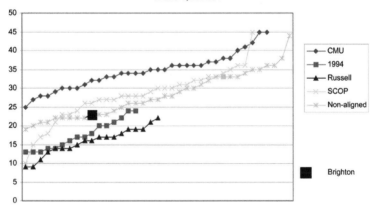

Figure 4.6 UK HE: recruitment by social class
Source: UUK (2003: 29)

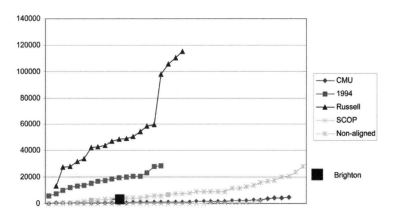

Figure 4.7 UK HE: public funding of research
Source: UUK (2003: 41)

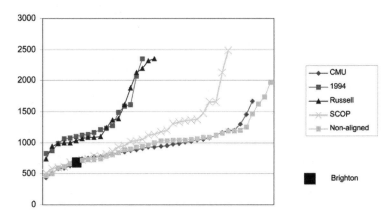

Figure 4.8 UK HE: administrative costs
Source: UUK (2003: 43)

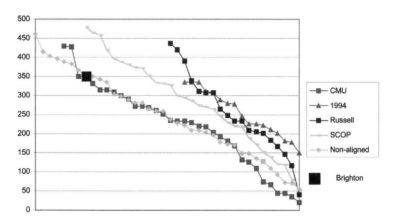

The Security Index, 2000/01

Figure 4.9 UK HE: financial security
Source: UUK (2003: 39)

views about HEFCE's locus in offering such guidance (OECD IMHE-
HEFCE 2004: 4).

- Analyses of institutional practice usually written by a commissioned expert individual or organization. These tend to be less
ambivalent in purpose and more authoritative because they
represent the views of the author, who will usually have independent standing in the sector. Such reports, for example on
institutional learning and teaching, widening participation and
staffing strategies, offer a valuable source of indirect information
against which Brighton has compared itself and which have helped
to inform its own thinking (see for example HEFCE 2001b, 2001c;
OPM 2002).

- Documentation from those institutions in receipt of project
funding under the Good Management Practice initiative. In addition to the HEFCE dissemination, these are often manifested in
individual websites and are inevitably somewhat variable, partly
because they reflect local enthusiasms and partly because they
were designed to be exploratory. But a number of them certainly
represent examples of collaborative institutional self-study that
should not go unnoticed and some have produced useful 'kits' and
other materials for use by other institutions.

External engagement

As well as using these data to inform understanding of itself, in context as well as over time, the intelligent institution will want to engage in debates about how analyses are constructed and used by other agencies. This requires some organized statistical expertise to enable routine modelling and testing, and participation in sector debates about techniques: for example, with the funding bodies about the development of performance indicators and definitional changes in the main data returns. To be fair, HEFCE and HESA do consult quite widely on possible changes and sometimes these can be 'pushed' by the sector. One example is the change in the construction of the benchmarks for the widening participation performance indicators used by the funding councils. Work by Brighton and others, including London Metropolitan University, demonstrated the fallacy of a benchmark that took no account of institutional location, and the more recent PIs now include a 'locationally adjusted benchmark' as well as an original benchmark that takes account of the pattern of subjects and entry qualifications.

Equally, an effective data cycle will enable the institution to make good use of data to contribute to substantive policy debates. For example, a focused use of the three UUK Longer Term Strategy Group reports described above at national level would enable recognition of some facts about the sector that could otherwise be overlooked, and that should be borne in mind not only in institutional planning but in higher education policy. Here are three examples:

- Changes in the pattern of student choices between subjects is not reflected in changes in the pattern of supply, with, in some cases, 'new entrant' institutions electing to offer subjects where overall student demand is falling significantly.
- The expected multiplier effect of high funding council research income leading to high research income from other sources is not proven. The 'gearing' effect of increased selectively or concentration in QR funding appears to have become dysfunctional (see also Watson 2003a: 1.2.1).
- Much of the contribution to sector diversity and to a number of key government objectives comes from the 'non-aligned' institutions, which tend to be overlooked in the tensions between the vocal research interests of the Russell and 94 Groups on the one hand and the espoused wider participation interests of the CMU on the other.

We noted earlier that an effective data cycle will also enable the institution to make good use of other external data sets. This will include not only those about UK higher education, but some important contextual data such as the Census, local data from the Index of Deprivation, data about local school achievements, international higher education data and information about sector and local skills requirements. Brighton, like many other institutions, has invested increasing effort in understanding these data and deploying them in evidence, for example when putting together funding proposals that require reference to particular dimensions of need. For instance, like other 'lead institutions' for the AimHigher widening participation initiative, the university used 'polar' data from HEFCE alongside data from the local education authorities on the take-up of free school meals and school achievements, and Census data on local deprivation, to identify priorities and frame intervention strategies.

Measuring performance

We said at the start of this chapter that a key purpose of the data cycle is to support evaluation of performance by the institution itself. There is a clear tension here, between well-known reservations about the extent to which higher education performance can be captured in digestible and reliable indicators, and the growing pressure to do so, whether from the impact of newspaper league tables or from institutional Boards or Councils.

The HEFCE-sponsored series of **performance indicators** on behalf of the UK funding bodies now includes a well-established and largely accepted set of data addressing the funding body's policy concerns. A number of universities are trying to create suites of performance analyses, whether based on the HEFCE data or using alternative sources. There are long-standing sensitivities here: PIs

> represent a very simple and compelling idea. They are measures of how well something is being done. But beyond this simple definition lie many complicated issues regarding who defines the goals and criteria for performance, who uses these indicators and for what purposes, and the many technical issues that surround any measurement effort.
>
> (Borden and Botrill 1994: 6)

The institution seeking to enhance its self-study faces some technical and political cautions in developing a suite of PIs for itself, or in using the funding council version uncritically. First, there is the technical specification – PIs should be 'readable, relevant and responsive' (Burke *et al.* 2002: 25) and provide 'a numerical value used to measure something which is difficult to quantify' (Cave *et al.* 1997: 21). The main weakness here is that PIs tend to focus on inputs and outputs, not processes or the relationship between the two. Indeed, a common failing is where PIs deal only with outputs, and are rendered meaningless once differences in inputs are taken into account (Johnes and Taylor 1990).

Secondly, there is a problematic relationship between what is being measured and what the institution is trying to do. Externally generated PIs will almost inevitably relate poorly to the specific aspirations of the individual university – 'a measure or statistic becomes a performance indicator [only] when it is explicitly associated with a goal or objective' (Borden and Bottrill 1994: 11). This can render them ambiguous, at best, and misleading at worst, depending on institutional context and/or mission. They also tend to be disconnected from the internal life of institutions 'where most of the performance occurs' (Burke *et al.* 2002: 23), with advocates not understanding 'the complexity of the institutional process' (Heywood 2000: 65), or being hostile to them (Johnes and Taylor [1990] on Jarratt [1985]). They tend to focus on accountability and control rather than organizational learning. They carry the danger of driving managers to focus on what is counted and therefore on the priorities of the body requiring the count, sometimes with deeply counterproductive 'reductionist' methodologies (Kells 1992: 56). These include an unhealthy obsession with league tables, which renders them susceptible to manipulation (Gater 2002) and can therefore distort and subvert what HEIs do. We comment further on the weaknesses of the **league table** approach and its impact in the UK and US in Chapter 8.

The HEFCE-led PIs reflect much sector-led work since the mid-1980s. They go some way to address some of these sorts of concerns and have succeeded in providing for the first time a set of reasonably robust data offering institutions some useful points of comparison. They use data provided by the institutions themselves, thus being more difficult to criticize on grounds of accuracy, while also giving back something of value in return for the pain of data collection. The funding council PIs look at aspects of widening participation, a particular measure of retention, and a particular measure of efficiency (HEFCE 1999). However, concerns remain: in particular, it is obvious that the PIs are unambiguously those of the funding councils and relate to *their* objectives (and probably more to the English funding council, post devolution, than to other territories) rather than necessarily to those of an individual institution.

Advocates of **benchmarking** claim that, while less well developed and less common than PIs (certainly if we look beyond metric benchmarking), it can address most if not all of the criticisms of PIs (Jackson and Lund 2000). Benchmarking is 'fundamentally an approach to self-evaluation through comparative analysis for the purposes of self-improvement' (Jackson and Lund 2000: 5). It is argued to be more powerful than PIs; better geared to learning; and better directed at the institution's own objectives. Jackson offers a useful summary of theoretical approaches as well as a number of UK higher education examples, but it is notable that most of these examples are about specific aspects of activity and service delivery rather than whole institutional approaches (Jackson 2002).

'Pure' benchmarking involves defining desired outputs, selecting what is to be benchmarked, identifying who is best at delivering these activities or outputs, collecting and analysing relevant data about processes and practices in the 'home' and benchmark institutions; and taking steps to close any performance gap that is identified (Watson 1993). But this is still problematic. Such an approach is labour-intensive and therefore costly; it implies agreement about what constitutes good practice between the benchmarking partners; and it implies a strong dose of both competition *and* of collaboration, through collaborative partnerships, likely to be difficult to navigate. However, a small number of 'benchmarking clubs' are now developing in the sector, including internationally, although of course international efforts need to take particular account of contextual differences (see for example the account of the CHEMS Club: Commonwealth Higher Education Management Service) (Fielden and Carr 2000). In addition, a number of the HEFCE-funded good management practice exercises have been strongly collaborative, enabling participating institutions to compare themselves on the particular activities, but on the premise that the institutions are learning together (and sharing the results with the sector more widely), rather than comparing themselves with 'best in class'.

There are two common uses of benchmarks in the performance context in the UK that fall short of the 'pure' variety implied here. First, the funding councils have constructed a set of technical benchmarks to accompany their PIs and help interpretation of them. These 'adjusted sector benchmarks' (ASB) are not strictly benchmarks in the sense described above since they do not represent a real institution, but a statistical construct that takes account of the entry and subject profile of the institution, as well as from where its students are drawn. In effect, this offers a view of what might reasonably be expected of the institution on each indicator, given what it offers and (in the case of the widening participation indicators) where it is located. Judgements about performance can therefore be placed in the context of the difference between the benchmark and achievement as well as achievement overall. This is perhaps an example of 'the political realization that benchmarking has the potential to promote change in line with a range of social and economic agendas' (Jackson 2002: 16).

Secondly, many institutions make straightforward use of published data to draw comparisons. This stops short of trying to 'get inside' any specific comparator institution to see how it works. It would be relatively unusual now to find a university that does not routinely compare itself on certain dimensions with chosen others, for example against national averages, others in their 'family group', or those with which they feel they compete.

The University of Brighton engages in this second more limited form of benchmarking, by preparing a series of **indicators of performance for the Board of Governors**, launched in October 2001. In this series, the Board receives reports about aspects of performance by the university alongside that of a group of eleven comparator institutions. This group includes those with similar missions and characteristics to the University of Brighton, as well as those close to it at present in most league tables; a 'traditional' university within Brighton's aspirational range; a different sort of 'new' university; those to which significant numbers of Brighton applicants also apply; and the university's nearest neighbour. The intention is to illuminate key aspects of activity and achievement, using published data. For each area of activity, some key indicators are presented together with a commentary that identifies similarities and differences in the data for Brighton, the sector average and the comparator group. Where possible, a short time series is included and links drawn between the indicator and the University's corporate plan aspirations. This approach is illustrated in Table 4.3.

This component of the data cycle has some strengths and weaknesses. Strengths include:

- using published and hence verified data;
- adopting a consistent set of comparator institutions;
- attempting coverage of most of the major areas of activity, including indicators of volumes; resource management; quality; market standing; student characteristics;
- relating the data where possible to the university's 'indicators of success' in the Corporate Plan.

But the weaknesses remain significant. They include:

Table 4.3 University of Brighton: indicators of performance for the Board of Governors

Comparator institutions	Aspects of performance

Bournemouth
Brunel
Kingston
London Metropolitan (formerly North London)
Oxford Brookes
Plymouth
Portsmouth
Sheffield Hallam
Staffordshire
Sussex
West of England
	• student characteristics including
	  • widening participation
	  • retention
	  • graduate destinations
	• financial performance
	• library efficiency and effectiveness
	• estate management, efficiency, space utilization
	• teaching quality
	• research quality, grants and contracts
	• popularity amongst applicants
	• overall size, shape and relative growth

- using published data means that these are sometimes quite dated when presented;
- the data will not always apply directly to institutional objectives, reducing the power of the comparisons;
- the Board knows little of the context in which members of the comparator group operate and therefore how to 'read' a particular indicator; while
- too often, the data prompt the response 'how interesting', while not obviously suggesting whether the performance illustrated is good or bad;
- the university has not to date extended its approach to engaging in collaborative work with the institutions identified to look in any detail at process or quality enhancement.

One of the purposes of the indicators of performance for the Brighton Board is to try to make sure that attention is focused on a broad range of aspects of performance, not just the obvious financial measures. A number of institutions in the US, and increasingly in the UK, have adopted the **balanced scorecard** to help them achieve a comprehensive and coherent overview of their performance. Like the two quality models considered in Chapter 5, the balanced scorecard has its origins in the private sector. It also has strong advocates of its capacity to underpin institutional performance because it is said to balance backward-looking financial indicators with the forward-looking attention on business processes, outputs, outcomes and learning, based on facts (Kaplan and Norton 1992; Balanced Score-card Institute 2004).

In higher education, a number of UK universities are using the balanced scorecard to provide a conceptual frame to their efforts to assess their performance (see for example University of Edinburgh 2004).

Market intelligence

One edition of the University of Brighton's indicators of performance series described earlier seeks to address the university's standing in the market, typically an area in which Board members are particularly interested but (as we saw in Chapter 2) left unsatisfied by the answers proffered. Most of the obvious 'measures' have flaws – for example, the ratio of applicants to enrolments, commonly used as a proxy for popularity, falls down where potential applicants self-screen, notoriously in the case of Oxbridge, but also in Brighton's own art and design provision and for the Brighton and Sussex Medical School, and for many courses at other institutions. The alternative, of seeking first-hand encounters with large numbers of applicants (let alone non-applicants) to gauge their opinions, is extremely expensive and methodologically difficult.

To complement the very basic information available on a comparative basis, the university has invested effort in the data cycle to improve the capacity to assess its popularity amongst aspiring students. The intention is to assist the planning process by informing a better match between courses offered and student demand; to understand the university's standing in the undergraduate market; and to make sure that the university is positioning itself appropriately in the offers it makes. To this end, its routine tools, centrally delivered electronically to Heads of School, now include a suite that draws on the large UCAS data sets combined with a series of mathematical applications developed in-house. These are designed to analyse:

- how applicants travel through the applications cycle, the points at which they drop out and reasons why applications turn into enrolments (or not) (heavily influenced by work at Kingston University);
- current year applications throughout the applications cycle and modelling changes at a point in time from previous years; and
- retrospective data on applications across the sector by subject.

In addition:

• analyses are available to Heads of School on the basis of requests that identify the other institutions to which Brighton applicants tend to apply in particular subjects (Appendix 1 2001c and 2003b);
• routine reports are presented on trends in GCSE and A/AS level entries;
• new courses are systematically reviewed after their first or second year to assess how stable their position is in the market, using data on applications and alternative choices by Brighton applicants as well as other intelligence on overall demand and competitor behaviour. This helps to inform decisions about relative growth and the 'price' to be asked in terms of the entry requirements for undergraduate programmes.

The final piece of information in the market intelligence armoury is the pair of annual surveys of new students and those who have declined an offer of an undergraduate place, which assess their reasons and perceptions (Appendix 1 2002b, 2003d, 2003e, 2004d).

Drawbacks remain – most of these accounts apply only to undergraduate entry and they tend to use data from a previous year. They are therefore arguably more about managing risk than underpinning a precise fit between supply and demand. However, the various sources of data do offer the prospect for some basic triangulation and this is now being refined in discussion with Heads of School, to ensure that the subject dimension is fully taken into account.

Reporting on progress

A key feature of each of the three major self-study cycles – data, planning and quality – is the component that reports on progress. In the data cycle, this focuses on assessing performance. The university has adopted a broad interpretation of 'performance measurement' that seeks to relate its approach to its own objectives. Here is the account offered in its self-evaluation document (SED) prepared for the institutional audit in May 2004:

> Each of the University's planning documents includes clearly stated targets and progress against them is subject to reflective monitoring. FABs [Faculty Academic Boards], ADC [Academic Development Committee] and Academic Board 'sign off' the plans and strategies and review progress against them. This cycle culminates in a review and assessment by the Board of

Governors of progress against the annual operating statement each summer. In addition, the University's published annual report provides a self-critical evaluation of progress in each area of the corporate plan, including numerical indicators drawing on published data where appropriate.

The Board of Governors also receives regular reports comparing aspects of the University's performance against those of a set of comparator institutions, for example, on application trends, or student characteristics.

In addition, the University has developed a number of survey-based reviews of aspects of performance, including surveys of student finances, reasons for choosing to study at Brighton, and reasons for leaving before qualification. Finally, the University requires schools and faculties to comment annually on their academic performance during the academic health process...

The University is therefore monitoring its progress:

- against its own objectives
- over time
- against published benchmarks in the HEFCE Performance Indicators
- against that of other universities
- using an emerging cycle of data analysis and performance measurement
- by comparing schools internally, against each other, against the university average and against their own objectives.

While the extent and power of the various data analyses has increased recently, the University does not use these simplistically. The committee structure ensures open discussion and informed judgement...

With respect to monitoring progress, the University is currently developing its 'data cycle' to embrace the components described here and to sit alongside its planning cycle. Already, in addition to the information about specific planned objectives, data on a number of themes are made available to Deans, Heads of School and others, to aid decision making and to improve the quality of debate and practice.

(Appendix 1 2004a: 28–9)

Some of this can be brought together in a schematic way by working through the key indicators, where the institution stands currently, where it wishes to move to, how progress can be measured, and whether information is available about relevant other institutions. One way in which a university might seek to do this is illustrated in Table 4.4 while Table 3.1 has shown the University of Brighton's aims and indicators.

Table 4.4 University of Brighton: measuring performance

Indicator	Current achievement	Strategic objective and desired achievement	Metric/data or evidence source	Comparative data
Volume of delivery	Numbers of students by mode/level/ funding source/ subject area	Desired size and shape of the institution; increases/ decreases in each category	As per HESA returns	Yes – HESA volumes (implicit time lag)
Research activity	Numbers of PhD students enrolled; completion rates; number of registered staff supervisors; number and value of research grants and contracts; funding council and research council grant; RAE outcomes	Desired changes in these	HESA and research activity survey; research management function; RAE	Yes – in part, HESA and sometimes annual reports; HEFCE circulars on funding allocations
Quality of provision	TQA assessment (but dated); student satisfaction; retention rates; perceptions of quality as indicated by application rates; employability data	Desired standing	TQA assessments; internal subject reviews; student feedback; institutional audit; complaints as proxy for satisfaction; retention PIs; first destinations data; external examiners' reports	Yes – TQA assessments and institutional audits, first destinations data; more information will become available via HERO and student feedback; published PIs

Indicator	Current achievement	Strategic objective and desired achievement	Metric/data or evidence source	Comparative data
Student characteristics	Proportions from different populations, regions etc.	Desired changes in these	HEFCE PIs; internal data on area of origin	Yes – HEFCE PIs on socio-economic characteristics
Effective partnerships	Progression rates from partner schools and colleges; enrolments on joint courses; other activities carried out jointly	Desired changes in these, process and outcome	Internal management information; possibly institutional audit	Not readily
Community engagement	Student volunteering	Desired strength and depth of engagement	Likely to be largely anecdotal/ descriptive	Difficult
Commercial activity	Percentage and amount of 'third stream' income	Desired increase	Management information	Limited – from published accounts
Financial security	Cash days in hand; surplus/ deficit; balance of funding council to other funding; overhead recovery	Desired position	Internal management information and finance record	Yes – from published accounts and HESA finance record
Operating efficiency	Overhead recovery rates; use of space; balance of planned to unplanned maintenance	Desired position	Internal management information, finance record, estates management statistics	Yes – as above but data on operating costs is patchy

This table suggests some 'hits' and some 'misses'. The biggest 'hit' is probably that it *is* possible to construct a set of data that tells you something in quantifiable terms about progress against some important institutional objectives, and that, at least in some cases, can be augmented with comparative data. However, there remain significant 'misses': the scope for drawing comparisons is limited by the published data; in some important areas, we have to rely on highly imperfect proxies, notably on the quality of provision and community engagement, and in others, progress will remain intangible (for example, the contribution of interpersonal relationships to effective partnership working).

In addition to using published data from large-scale data sets offering ostensibly objective information about the institution and the sector as a whole, the university commissions a number of surveys to improve its understanding of the experiences and views of the student and staff respondents. These can offer complementary – or confounding – knowledge. These are illustrated in Table 4.5.

Table 4.5 University of Brighton: surveys of students and staff

Subject and frequency	Scope	Illustrative findings	Findings considered by
Why students choose the University of Brighton and the decliners' survey (Appendix 1 2002b, 2003d, 2003e, 2004d) Annually	About 5,500 new students; response rate of nearly 50% for undergraduates and just over 50% for new postgraduates; plus about 3000 declining students with 17% response rate	• Increasing use and influence of the internet in students' decision making, with the university's website increasing in influence; • different factors that influence mature and young students and home/ EU and overseas students; • differences between university Schools in the proportion of students for whom they are the first or only choice; • continuing influence of the availability of the right course on students enrolling; • those enrolling and those declining share concerns about finance, accommodation and making friends; those declining are less likely to have visited the university, to find the university's information helpful or to believe the right course is available.	Academic Development Committee; Recruitment Group

Subject and frequency	Scope	Illustrative findings	Findings considered by
The financial situation of students at the University of Brighton (Appendix 1 2003g) Annually, since 1992	Full-time level two students using a cluster sampling method; nearly 500 responses (70%)	• Gradual increase in the acceptance by students of loans and of students taking financial responsibility for the costs of their studies, but combined with the majority view that high costs put off potential students from higher education; • more than half of students have regular paid employment during term time, with median earning of £65 a week, but at the same time, 64% of respondents believe that this adversely affects their studies; • more than half of respondents receive financial help from their families in addition to any assessed contribution and this percentage has increased steadily, with over a third now reporting that they had received £2,000 or more since starting their course; • just over one-third of students drive and just over one-third walk to the university; • expenditure patterns differ widely between groups of students, largely between the young living away from home and mature students, especially those with children; • the financial support available to students does not appear to meet the needs of significant numbers of students with family responsibilities; • nearly one-third of students remained in credit at this stage in their course but nearly 30% were £2,000 or more in debt;	Academic Board, Board of Governors

Subject and frequency	Scope	Illustrative findings	Findings considered by
		• patterns of debt differ between groups of students, with students with dependents and young students from low-income backgrounds accumulating more than average levels of debt.	
Work–life balance survey (Appendix 1: Cooper 2001) One-off, 2001	All staff, 764 respondents (45% response rate)	• 36% respondents have elder care responsibilities; 26% are primary carer; 10% have pre-school children; • 46% have academic or other positions of office; • positive views about informal support at work and about upward relationships; • high levels of perceived excess workload; • mixed views about flexible work arrangements, their impact on career and overall effectiveness.	Senior staff and with the Trades Unions
Organizational Character Index Survey (Appendix 1: Azure 2003) One-off, 2003 and 2004	Heads of School/ Department (in two cohorts)	• University relatively high on integrity and resilience, less high on distinctiveness (see Figure 9.6)	Senior staff, Board of Governors
Questionnaire to early leavers (Appendix 1 2004g) Throughout the year	Students who leave before completing their course	• The predominant reasons cited by students for leaving their course concern a mismatch between the course and their aspirations or expectations.	Student Retention Review Group
Surveys of service users (catering and information services) (Appendix 1 2003i, 2004h) Various but regular – information services annually	Catering – all staff and students (July and December 2002, 800 responses) Information services – all students (619 responses)	• High rates of satisfaction with catering standards and choice, 'average' satisfaction with value for money; • more up-to-date books and key texts as most important issues, followed by longer opening hours and easier access from home.	Functional committees (Learning Resources, Student Services)

Subject and frequency	Scope	Illustrative findings	Findings considered by
Student written submission (Appendix 1: University of Brighton Students' Union 2004) For Institutional Audit May 2004	All students invited to take part, over 470 responses	• High levels of satisfaction with teaching quality, learning support, books/journals, ICT, the estate, accuracy of course information and the prospectus, perceived value for money; • concerns about support while on placement, consistency of assessment, independence of complaints procedures.	Academic Board, including commentary on responses to concerns raised

Finally, the university attempts to bring together what it can glean from individual student complaints and appeals in an annual account to see whether there are any general issues or parts of the university where additional work needs to be done. Sometimes these can be revealing about aspects of process and systems, often revealing gaps in communication and understanding although, of course, the scale of the cases needs to be kept in perspective (Appendix 1 2003m).

All this is brought together in the **Annual Academic Year Review** and the **Annual Academic Health Report**, prepared for consideration by the Academic Board. These parallel and complementary analyses offer a comprehensive overview of provision and of progress. The Annual Academic Year Review is a detailed account by administrative function of largely quantitative aspects of delivery, including student applications and enrolments; use of the various parts of Student Services including demands for counselling and financial support services; and the results of the function-related user surveys described above. It complements the Annual Academic Health Report, a key element in the university's quality process, which we discuss in more detail in Chapter 5. The Annual Academic Year Review allows (and expects) Heads of Department to stand back from the daily responsibility of service delivery and reflect on the quality of work, changes in the pattern of demand for their service, achievement against targets, and to identify issues to be addressed in the coming year. In so doing, they draw on the various sources of data described here including any specialist 'user surveys' relevant to their department as well as changes in the policy and practice context.

The main morals of the data cycle are: that information is vital, but also slippery – it has to be sought with energy, but also used with sophistication; and that it means nothing unless and until it is interpreted. These are all lessons well understood by social scientists; they often have to be learned by institutional managers.

5

THE QUALITY CYCLE

This book is about how self-study can assist the enhancement of quality across the range of activities of universities and colleges. This chapter explores in more detail how an institution can build an effective quality cycle and better understand the quality of what it does. It concentrates on the quality of learning and teaching, in the context of the continuing debate about external quality assurance regimes and the international interest in comparative quality assessment frameworks.

Doing quality management well is important: it 'has become a central mechanism in the management of institutional change in higher education' (Brennan and Shah 2000: 87). But the same authors note that it is intrinsically difficult: 'at its most effective, quality assessment is about learning and about sharing the lessons of that learning. It is about crossing boundaries, about constructing bridges, about confronting vested interests, about accepting change as seen through critical and sometimes sceptical eyes' (Brennan and Shah 2000: 140).

Quality assurance in UK higher education

We noted in Chapter 1 the political dimension to self-study, deriving from the culture of the individual institution and of the context of higher education more generally. This comes into sharp focus when considering the quality cycle.

Quality assurance of UK higher education presents some painful historical ironies. The UK system is admired around the world for its commitment to systematic peer review. At home, the 'quality wars' have threatened to tear the sector apart. As UK higher education grew, from the early nineteenth century onwards, new frameworks were developed through which the national academic community took responsibility for its own enlargement. 'Validating' universities, 'external' degrees, and external membership of university and university college committees played their part in the late nineteenth and early twentieth centuries, before the late-twentieth century phases of expansion, overseen by 'academic advisory committees' for the new Robbins foundations and the Council for National Academic Awards (CNAA) for what was 'public sector' higher education. Meanwhile the sector as a whole has underwritten the distinctive 'British' arrangements for assurance of standards by external examiners.

Following the Conservative reforms of the late 1980s and 1990s, these were increasingly bound up in national organizations: the funding councils' quality assessment committees and the sector's own bodies like the Higher Education Quality Council (HEQC) and Quality Assurance Agency for Higher Education (QAA). Simultaneously, and just as the world was beating a path to the British door to learn how to do it, confidence eroded and institutional resentment reached its peak (Watson and Taylor 1998: 74–9). So the national frameworks with which self-study has to contend remain both contentious and unstable.

An institutional decision about what sort of quality cycle will best assist its overall objectives for assuring and enhancing the quality of what it does will answer two very practical questions – what works and what is acceptable? But it can only do so by understanding the particular nature of the university enterprise. Universities are, famously, 'loosely coupled, diverse, complex and sometimes inscrutable organizations' (Kells 1992: 50). They have a peculiarly intimate relationship between self-assessment and the delivery of an externally credible guarantee of standards in which the producers necessarily have a major stake in the processes of interrogation (Barnett 1994: 167). In this context, 'relatively reductionist performance indicators and obtrusive inspection tend to dampen enthusiasm for, and even extinguish, the most valuable aspects of regulation – those conducted within the organization and intent on improvement' (Kells 1992: 56–7).

Both the data and planning cycles need to take account of external requirements – not only because these are frequently non-negotiable but also because they can offer useful guides to the institution. Nonetheless, there have been some hard-fought debates about the locus of those requirements, their nature and impact, as we show in Chapters 4 and 6. Designing and operating a quality cycle within the broader self-study effort takes place in the middle of even more intense debates about the nature and purpose of systems to assure and assess quality and standards. Typical questions include the following:

- should systems be driven by self-evaluation or by external accountability?
- who should be involved in making assessments of quality?
- is the primary purpose continuous improvement or stakeholder satisfaction?
- how can innovation and risk be managed in the context of safeguarding standards?
- is the predominant mode retrospective or prospective, to assure or to enhance?

This is complex stuff: a 'mélange of differential power and purposes and ... resulting multitude of forms of quality evaluation', constituting 'a new language of higher education' (Barnett 1994: 83 and 84). The search for a workable sector-wide system has been one of the dominant debates in higher education over the last two decades in the UK, manifested in a succession of reviews and evolving frameworks. These frameworks have been influenced by views about the implications for quality and standards of sustained expansion, and also now by territorial perceptions, with different systems applying in England and Scotland, and a high degree of sensitivity about what is called the 'Welsh dimension'.

All this points to a highly contested terrain. In the climate of public and publicized institutional audit reports, and the rhetoric if not the reality of providing meaningful information to students and other stakeholders, the stakes are high – with quality management causally related to 'future institutional success, and even survival' (Brennan and Shah 2000: 87).

In the midst of these debates, we argue that institutions with a strong capacity for self-study will be better placed to meet quality assurance requirements, whether internal or external, and also to improve their own practice.

Behind the practical questions, therefore, lie questions of intent. Barnett offers a useful taxonomy for looking at any particular method of evaluation, which relates method to purpose:

- fitness for purpose or measurement against a standard;
- summative or formative evaluation;
- accountability or self-learning;
- quality control or assurance;

- criterion or norm referencing;
- customer satisfaction or producer norms.

(Summarized from Barnett 1994: 84–5)

Barnett goes on to suggest that modes of evaluation can be considered on two axes, 'enlightenment' and 'power', and that the dominant trend is for a shift from modes characterized by collegiality and self-enlightenment to modes characterized by the bureaucratic and technicist, such that 'a realm of hermeneutic transactions (the academy) is becoming colonised by a technicism linked to purposive knowledge interests rooted in surveillance, control and external direction' (Barnett 1994: 94).

Implicit in Barnett's framework are the respective interests of the state, market and academic institutions. Brennan and Shah, commenting on the institutions taking part in the Organisation for Economic Cooperation and Development (OECD) Programme on Institutional Management in Higher Education (IMHE), note the continuing importance of accountability to the academic community (Brennan and Shah 2000: 86–7). Nonetheless, concern about a shift towards external influences dominating modes of quality evaluation is part of conventional wisdom in both Europe and the US, and is arguably a response both to increasing student numbers and to changing understandings of the role of higher education in broader social and economic developments. In this context, states push for a shift away from an interest in the way institutions accredit and assure the awards made in their names and towards a steering mechanism in which the qualitative assessment of outputs becomes 'a tool for improving public services' (Dill 1998: 372). The consequence is the growth of the 'quality industry' noted by Tight (2003: 108), a special example of what is now regularly referred to as the 'audit society' (Power 1999). Alongside the need to articulate a proper place for the powerful interests of the state, however, there is a need to clarify who the customers are. In this respect, the UK is now following the international trend to seek ways of building student views and interests into any institutional quality cycle.

Some of this was played out in the 1997 Dearing Committee report: 'institutions of higher education and their staff have demonstrated great commitment to ensuring the quality of provision over the last decade, at a time of an expansion in student numbers unmatched by increases in funding. Indeed, the systems in the United Kingdom (UK) for assuring the quality of higher education provision are among the more rigorous in the world' (NCIHE 1997: 143). However, it went on to state that 'the system of external examiners alone cannot guarantee comparability of standards across a diverse mass system of higher education' (NCIHE 1997: 143), recommending benchmark standards for awards, an enhanced external examiner system, better information for students and employers, national codes of practice for institutions and a reformed complaints system for students.

The current formal external framework for an institutional quality cycle concerned with learning and teaching in England has eight main components, not counting the informal but no less powerful publication of league tables:

- institutional audit (QAA);
- academic discipline trails (QAA);
- continuing academic review of HE in FE (QAA);
- inspection of teacher training (Ofsted);
- professional and statutory body validation and accreditation (in relevant areas);
- external examination;
- performance indicators about student retention and achievement (HEFCE); and
- publication of information for students.

Institutional audit

The external requirements on institutions in England come in the form of the institutional audit process. The first audit visits took place in January 2003, replacing the previous practice of subject assessments. Institutional audit is designed to examine institutional quality assurance systems as well as their operation within academic disciplines and individual programmes of study. The audit is intended to promote and enhance high-quality learning and teaching, provide a basis for public accountability, ensure there is reliable information for students, employers and others, and provide a basis for improvement where this is necessary (QAA 2002b: 2).

Institutional audits result in a judgement about the extent to which there can be public confidence in 'the soundness of the institution's present and likely future management of the quality of its programmes and the academic standards of its awards' and 'the reliance that can reasonably be placed on the accuracy, integrity, completeness and frankness of the information that an institution published about the quality of its programmes and standard of its awards' (QAA 2002b: 4). Judgements can be of broad confidence, limited confidence or no confidence. To reach their judgement, audits examine three main areas:

- the effectiveness of an institution's internal quality assurance structures and mechanisms ... This provides public information on an institution's soundness as a provider of tertiary qualifications of national and international standing;
- the accuracy, completeness and reliability of the information that an institution publishes about the quality of its programmes and the standards of its awards ... This provides information on the trust that can be placed in an institution's own published descriptions of the quality of its provision...;
- several examples of the institution's internal quality assurance processes at work at the level of the programme ... or across the institution as a whole ... in order to demonstrate the validity and reliability of the information being generated by these internal processes...'

(QAA 2002b: 3)

These judgements can also be accompanied by commentaries on good practice or recommendations about areas that need more attention – actions that can be deemed 'essential', 'advisable' or 'desirable'. These institution-wide judgements are set against published advice to institutions in the form of the Framework for Higher Education Quality (FHEQ), a Code and a set of subject benchmark statements. Although the QAA does not take an explicitly risk-based approach to quality management, it does look particularly closely at areas of institutional activity that it regards as likely to be more risky – notably domestic and international collaborations, especially where they involve making awards in the institution's name.

On the Barnett taxonomy, the QAA approach appears to have a number of features, some of them potentially contradictory. On the one hand, the audit starts from a self-evaluation document (SED) in which institutions are invited to identify their strengths and weaknesses, possibly supplemented by a written submission from the students via their union. On the other, it appears that auditors are quite prepared to make judgements about institutions that imply a normative set of expectations, and to involve themselves in enhancement as much as in assurance.

Using external information

As with other data published about the sector, the intelligent university will learn from published audit reports about other institutions and from other sources when thinking about the structure, operation and effectiveness of its own quality cycle.

QAA has published a useful summary of issues from the first eight institutional audit reports (QAA 2003a). Several areas of good practice are noted – student support and the student learning experience, student representation in quality assurance procedures, and staff support and development. However, they also contain a number of recommendations about the operation of aspects of institutions' quality assurance frameworks; their articulation and operation of roles and responsibilities; collecting and using relevant information to inform decisions; and about the scope of the quality cycle. Many of these are about making the right choice about the institution's approach; how systematic the institution is in doing what it sets out to do; whether it has and makes use of an adequate information base; and whether it 'closes the loop'. Table 5.1 illustrates some of the commendations and recommendations from a selection of institutional audit reports published by the QAA up to early 2004 that are relevant to a quality cycle.

Table 5.1 Learning from institutional audit

Systematic collection and use of information about the quality of provision including to inform decisions
Commended   • A detailed university-wide investigation into undergraduate performance and the factors affecting degree classification; effective online system for monitoring student performance [Cambridge];   • data analysis pointing to an emerging problem of student retention, including comparisons with other institutions, coupled with a strong diagnostic system to identify individual students who may need additional support [School of Oriental and African Studies (SOAS)].
Recommended   • Ensure that responses to internal and external reviews are timely and followed up, including handling reports from external examiners [SOAS];   • review scope of upward reporting so that central committees can have an effective institutional oversight of quality assurance and enhancement [Liverpool];   • make more systematic and proactive use of data about student progression and achievement to monitor student progress from admissions to completion [Royal Northern College of Music (RNCM)]; ensure a management information system that can better reflect students' complex progression arrangements [Middlesex]; give priority to developing the management information system to give an effective tool to evaluate student progression and achievement [Lincoln] and to support academic functions [Royal Academy of Music (RAM)].

Clarity of roles, responsibilities and decision-making processes

Recommended
- Identify senior strategic responsibility to manage quality and standards and a process to systematically track and respond to issues raised by students and external examiners [London Business School (LBS)];
- strengthen effectiveness of dissemination and implementation of centrally determined policies and procedure [Royal College of Art (RCA)];
- clarify managerial and academic decision-making processes so that routes by which issues are addressed are identified and the relevant staff involved [RNCM];
- make explicit executive functions, scope and extent of authority of committees for achievement of learning and teaching targets [Liverpool];
- review respective roles and responsibilities of the components of its formal system [Institute of Education (IE)].

Systems to inform practice with student feedback and engagement

Commended
- Student representation at all levels [RAM];
- a culture that is highly responsive to student views including evaluation data on electives from previous students, made available to inform current student choice, and rapid response to student feedback [LBS];
- active involvement of students in staff development for learning and teaching [Liverpool].

Recommended
- Ensure greater consistency in the arrangements for student representation and student feedback, including from past students [SOAS];
- define university-wide minimum requirements for qualitative feedback on student performance [York];
- development of a formal complaints procedure [LBS];
- develop arrangements for student participation in quality assurance processes [Bradford].

Informing current practice through external engagement and comparisons

Commended
- Effective engagement with Professional and Statutory Body (PSB) accreditation [Bradford];
- collaboration with the Victoria and Albert Museum giving students access to a unique resource [RCA];
- use of programme specifications to specify learning outcomes and assessment criteria [Lincoln].

Recommended
- Engage, learn from and contribute to UK higher education academy infrastructure [LBS];
- take a more strategic and self-critical approach to the management of quality and standards [RNCM].

Systems to support students

Commended
- Review of administrative services focusing on the student experience as a driver for quality enhancement [Essex];
- 24–7 website providing online information; environment in which needs and expectations of a diverse student population are met [Middlesex];
- system of academic and pastoral support sustaining the university's distinctive ethos [York];
- integrated approach to student support including website and handbook, responsive to need and effectively evaluated [Sheffield];
- systematic effort to provide individually tailored learning experience [RAM];
- Doctoral school framework for research students [IE];
- support for former students [RNCM].

Systems to develop good teaching practice

Commended
- Departmental contacts from the University Teaching Committee to facilitate ownership of policy and procedure, and the exchange of good practice [York];
- the network of educational development roles [Southampton];
- the role of prize-winners in contributing to training for other staff [Liverpool];
- systems for staff induction and mentoring, development and promotion [Middlesex]; induction and mentoring for new staff [Bradford];
- use of investment funds to support developmental and enhancement projects [Essex].

Systems to handle risk

Commended
- Systems to promote continuous improvement in collaborative provision [Liverpool];
- systems to ensure the quality of work-based learning [Middlesex].

Recommended
- Amend format of annual reporting statements to ensure explicit reporting of franchised and accredited programmes; implement fully the framework to ensure standards in international accredited programmes [Southampton];
- review Committee practices to ensure information necessary to assure

the quality and standards of awards offered in conjunction with other bodies [Cambridge];
- review processes to ensure effective oversight of collaborative provision [Bradford];
- review assessment practices to underpin transparency consistency and fairness [Sheffield];
- define institution-wide criteria for pass/borderline/fail performance [RCA].

Source: QAA 2003c–2004

Other approaches ▄

We have noted already that the prevailing audit regime in England is not the only approach to evaluating the quality of learning and teaching. Practice in Scotland, for example, emphasizes enhancement – and the management of enhancement – which is much more explicitly defined as 'improving the effectiveness of student learning, seeking to learn from current activities, reference points and good practice, and to make the most effective use of resources to support learning' (QAA 2003b: 3). A thorough, workable and useful quality cycle will be no more constrained by the requirements of the QAA than an effective data cycle is defined by the collection of data to meet HESA obligations or a planning cycle by the requirements of HEFCE. The canny institution will design and implement cycles that simultaneously meet external as well as internal needs.

We noted in Chapter 1 the strength of advocacy of effective organizational learning as the key to organizational success. In designing a quality cycle, it is worth noting the work of those who advocate quality management with similar passion. The development and promotion of formal models to achieve this has taken hold in the private sector following concerns about the 'cost of quality' in both the US and Europe and the perception that weaknesses in quality control practice explained inferior productivity and lack of international competitiveness. This reflects a fundamental shift in thinking:

> the external connotations of quality changed ... to reflect its indispensable role in corporate strategy formulations. It was seen, for the first time, as a formidable competitive weapon, that ... could make or break organizations.
>
> (Kumar and Douglas 2002: 31)

Two powerful models in popular use outside higher education are increasingly being explored by colleges and universities, albeit more in the US than the UK. Both are based on the idea of business excellence – that there is a business 'ideal' against which the individual organization can be compared or can compare itself. Both have recently been adapted for use beyond the firm – in one case to refer specifically to the public sector and in the other specifically to education. These are the Excellence Model from the European Foundation for Quality Management (EFQM) and the US Baldrige National Quality Program (BNQP) (EFQM 2002; BNQP 2004). Big claims are made particularly for the BNQP, whose adherents are said (at least until recently) to significantly out-perform conventional stock market trackers (NIST 2002). The take-up of, and apparent enthusiasm for, the EFQM Model has been impressive: a survey for the Cabinet Office in 2000 showed that the Model was being used by over 20,000 organizations across Europe, and that within the UK over 80 per cent of the public sector users surveyed reported that it was an effective tool (Pricewaterhouse Coopers, quoted in Cabinet Office [undated]). It also has some powerful advocates: 'in the jungle that is quality improvement, the Model is the biggest beast ... It is an approach therefore that the whole of the public sector should consider' (Pricewaterhouse Coopers, quoted in Cabinet Office [undated]). The Cabinet Office subsequently concluded that 'the Government's view ... is that the Model is the most effective tool for achieving improvement, and ultimately excellence across the whole range of an organisation's activities' (Cabinet Office [undated]).

BNQP and EFQM have some features in common relevant to an effective quality cycle. They emphasize the importance of:

- institutional leadership;
- mission specificity;
- the relationship between process and outcome;
- non-financial as well as financial outcomes;
- systematic self-evaluation;
- ongoing improvement in a virtuous circle;
- stakeholder views, including students, staff and other communities.

Advocates argue that using one or other of these models has a number of benefits, providing:

- rigour and structure to underpin continuous improvement – the BNQP in particular incorporates a concept of excellence as value-added performance with two components: '(1) year-to-year improvement in key measures and indicators of performance, especially student learning, and (2) demonstrated leadership in performance and performance improvement relative to comparable organizations and to appropriate benchmarks' (BNQP 2004: 9);

- judgements about achievement based on facts and evidence;
- a powerful diagnostic tool focusing energy on areas where improvement is most needed and where real savings in operating costs can be made;
- staff involvement across the institution, for example through questionnaires about their perceptions;
- a clearly articulated relationship between the institution's own objectives and the means to achieve them;
- focus on the quality of learning and teaching – 'your organization should view itself as a key developmental influence on students ... and ... should seek to understand and optimize its influencing factors' (BNQP 2004: 9);
- a feedback loop, via the emphasis on 'institutional learning'; and
- an overarching framework that can support a '"joined up" performance management strategy' (Cabinet Office [undated]).

However, there are some downsides to the BNQP and the EFQM models. Critics argue that they are:

- prescriptive about the factors to be considered and their relative importance (for example in their scoring systems), although BNQP in particular seeks to relate judgements to institutional objectives;
- static rather than dynamic: 'while these frameworks provide an excellent snapshot of strengths and weaknesses of an organization at the time they are assessed, they do not have a built-in structure that will create or sustain an improvement momentum' (Kumar and Douglas 2002: 45);
- derived from models of competitive performance in the private sector where those requiring high performance from the organization can be defined non-contentiously as customers or shareholders, rather than the multiple stakeholders in higher education, and where outputs are relatively easy to define and measure;
- applicable only to a simplistic organizational model that sits poorly in a complex university setting where the emphasis is on effectiveness across a wide terrain;
- predicated on a largely hierarchical organizational model that assumes that change is relatively easily instituted;
- exhausting and daunting to carry out – use of the full EFQM framework would involve the institution in addressing some 1,500 questions about itself; and
- not easily reconciled with the need within higher education to

address both judgements directed at determining thresholds (for the standard and comparability of the awards made) and activity directed at enhancement.

In higher education, EFQM is used by HEFCE as part of its internal management and is also the focus of one of the Good Management Projects that HEFCE has sponsored in the sector. It is being explored by some twenty HEIs. However, as Tight notes, there remains room for more comparative research into the respective benefits of different quality assessment systems (Tight 2003: 119).

Within the sector, alongside the QAA framework described earlier, HEFCE has encouraged the development of learning and teaching strategies through identifying specific funding for enhancement. This approach includes a helpful good practice guide as well as an expert externally authored analysis of the early progress in strategy development in this area (HEFCE 2001c, 2001d). The latter noted the need for alignment between the learning and teaching strategy and other activities (such as estates, widening participation and information technology strategies). It commented that, while there had been significant improvements in approach (notably in including student feedback, in setting targets and evaluating progress and in supporting innovation), nonetheless 'institutions have a considerable way to go to join up their strategic thinking and to have fully integrated learning and teaching strategies' (HEFCE 2001d: 7).

In parallel, work is ongoing to explore risk-based approaches to quality assurance, which, as we have seen, is implicit in the QAA's approach. The issue here is about the balance between experimentation and standards. QAA notes of its work in Scotland:

> Enhancement is the result of change which may include innovation. Change and innovation will frequently involve risk. Institutions are required to manage this risk in a way that provides reasonable safeguards for current students. The review process will recognise and support effective risk management and adopt a supportive and not punitive role in this context.
>
> (QAA 2003b: 3)

One of the HEFCE-funded good management practice projects investigated a risk-based approach to quality and argues that such an approach could both reduce costs and help shift from assurance to enhancement (Raban and Turner 2003).

The quality framework

Like most universities, Brighton makes implicit and explicit reference to quality in its mission and aims – its mission states that it will 'secure the best possible outcomes for its students, staff and partners' and one of its aims is to 'secure an extensive, challenging and high quality academic portfolio by combining assured standards with flexibility of response' (Appendix 1 2003b: 4) It makes reference in the Corporate Plan to the distinctive quality of learning and teaching and, as we set out in Table 3.1, includes amongst its indicators of success reference to subject reviews, institutional audits of partner colleges, engagement in sectoral quality assurance and completion of its own QAA institutional audit.

The self-evaluation document (SED) describes the framework as 'designed to support the diversity and complexity of its academic community' and identifies three underpinning principles:

- critical self-reflection;
- external scrutiny and external accountability;
- collective ownership of quality and standards.

(Appendix 1 2004a: 21)

It further identifies four contributing activities:

- provision of information (both qualitative and quantitative) which is timely and consistent to inform academic planning and enhancement in courses, schools, faculties, central departments and the institution;
- documented procedures and processes to assure standards and ensure consistency across the University;
- appropriately resourced policies and strategies which provide the necessary underpinning to enhance teaching and support learning; and
- extensive use of external peer review in internal processes and including the use of national benchmarks, professional body and accreditation agency criteria to assure the national standing of awards.

(Appendix 1 2004a: 21–2)

The framework has a number of components that help assure standards and provide a basis for quality enhancement at different levels. The framework is illustrated in Table 5.2.

Table 5.2 University of Brighton: the quality framework

Level	Supported by	Use
Individual academic	Professional development; Centre for Learning and Teaching; subject centres; subject and professional engagement; peer observation of teaching; staffing strategy	Staff Development Review
Module	Common Academic Framework; student feedback	Annual Academic Health process – Academic Board
Course	PSB engagement and accreditation; academic and assessment regulations; course development handbook; external involvement; student feedback; progression and completion data	Accreditation
Learning and student support services	Student feedback; service review; data on usage; personal support and guidance; Learning and Teaching Strategy	Annual Academic Year Review – Academic Board
Institution	Student feedback; policies on equal opportunities, personal tutoring, peer observation of teaching, estates and information services; Learning and Teaching Strategy; leadership programme	Annual Academic Health process – Academic Board QAA institutional audit Reporting on progress of Learning and Teaching Strategy to HEFCE
Subject	Subject centres; disciplinary and professional networks (external involvement); internal subject review	QAA Disciplinary Engagement
Partner college	Staff development; memoranda of cooperation; disciplinary and professional networks (external involvement)	Annual Academic Health process – Academic Board; Partner College Review – Academic Partnership Committee

The quality cycle   ■

An effective quality cycle will make this framework dynamic, yielding insights into the quality of learning and teaching and ways in which they can be enhanced, drawing on information from relevant sources and using that to aid judgements about quality and decisions about provision and practice. There will be an intimate relationship between work to assure standards and work to enhance the quality of learning and teaching.

The University of Brighton identifies the ability to learn and adapt as central – we have already noted that the self-evaluation document prepared for the 2004 institutional audit identifies 'critical self-reflection' as one of the three key principles underpinning its approach to quality and standards. The SED makes a number of relevant claims: the university 'judges itself to be an academic community which is currently substantially achieving its academic objectives and which is sufficiently self-critical and reflective to be able to predict and avoid, or recognise and rectify, weaknesses and limitations in its academic provision and quality assurance system' and that 'actively cultivates an academic culture in which professional higher education teachers are encouraged, and expected, to undertake continuous self-reflection' (Appendix 1 2004a: 21 and 22). It concludes ambitiously:

> We acknowledge that, in common with most UK universities, a major and continuing challenge to the maintenance of quality and standards remains the amount and patterns of public, or publicly regulated, funding made available … Only a well-managed, self-confident, but properly self-critical institution will be in an effective position to meet this challenge. We judge ourselves to be such an institution.
>
> (Appendix 1 2004a: 88)

Like the data and the planning cycles, this sort of critical self-reflection needs both internal and external reference points. It derives externally from the perspectives of experts in the subject as well as professional and statutory bodies, and internally from detailed monitoring of delivery and the expertise of individual academics, other colleagues and the perspectives of students. These reference points apply at different levels, including the individual module, course and subject, as well as the institution. The purpose is to ensure both that the standards of awards are met and maintained and that the quality of learning and teaching is being enhanced.

With regard to standards, 'the University recognises three related, sometimes competing reference points:

- 'how course delivery and student performance equate to the course design and curriculum as validated;
- how the course compares to courses of the same award type within the University...;
- how the course compares to similar courses in that subject in other UK universities...'

(Appendix 1 2004a: 24)

The pattern of reference points is illustrated in simplified form in Figure 5.1.

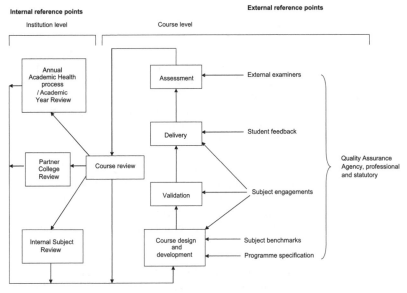

Figure 5.1 Internal and external reference points for critical self-reflection about learning and teaching

An effective quality cycle will share some of the characteristics of the data and planning cycles, in that it will be:

- carefully integrated with the other two formal self-study cycles, data and planning;
- organized and managed to optimize the fit between internal and external requirements: 'meeting standards should ideally form part

of a quality system which sees quality improvement as starting a chain reaction' (Liston 1999: 135);

• rooted in what the institution itself is trying to achieve, with an appropriate scope;
• sensitive to the balance and possible trade-off between effort and outcomes;
• integrated into the committee, decision-making and governance structures and processes, with clearly defined roles and responsibilities;
• informed by internal and external reference points; and
• capable of generating valid and relevant information for internal and external audiences.

In addition, an effective quality cycle needs to respect the particular facets of the university enterprise that we noted at the start of this chapter. It will therefore:

• recognize that it will not be possible to construct an evaluation that is value-free: 'all methods depend on certain value judgements' (Heywood 2000: 72) and institutional evaluation 'cannot be seriously accomplished as a value-free enquiry. Still less can it be conducted as a purely technical affair, weighing up specific means of evaluation' (Barnett 1994: 172). This requires the institution to define for itself what constitutes the quality of its activity, in the light of its own objectives;
• recognize that there is a particular problem about the sort of information required to draw sensitive and meaningful conclusions about quality: in some cases this just does not exist, not only because it could only be gathered over the long term but also because it is difficult to attribute effects to institutional causes (Romney *et al.* 1989, Kells 1995);
• be inclusive and properly collegial, aiming for participation 'that allows those with the responsibility to carry out changes to discover the need for those changes and to formulate them' (Kells 1995: 18); build upon a climate of trust that enables institutional conversation and can help to secure 'a process of collaborative critical enquiry' (Barnett 1992: 124); and result in the 'collective ownership of quality and standards' (Appendix 1 2004a: 21). This means that academics need to be engaged not only in the quality cycle of their own institution, but to be encouraged and enabled to engage in the quality processes of other institutions, national debates, and the work of relevant subject and professional bodies;
• find sensible ways of involving students and ascertaining and acting on their views; and

- enable innovation aimed at enhancement, while also minimizing the possible risk to assured standards.

The University's quality cycle is illustrated in Figure 5.2.

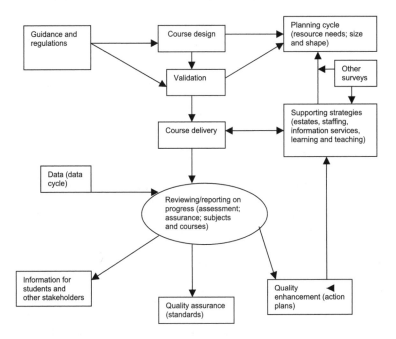

Figure 5.2 University of Brighton: the quality cycle

Involving students

We saw earlier that the QAA, Baldrige and EFQM frameworks all place considerable weight on involving students and listening to their views in both assuring standards and enhancing quality. This has to be done with some care. As the University's Corporate Plan notes, while the intention is to offer high-quality learning and teaching, the experience also has to be challenging (Appendix 1 2003a: 4). Meanwhile, as we noted earlier, the university has not followed some others, notably the University of Central England (UCE), in embracing student satisfaction as a reliable and central component of its quality cycle (Geall *et al.* 1997).

The policy framework for involving students in quality matters in the UK has been developed most recently under the auspices of the Task Group on Information on Quality and Standards in Higher Education, chaired by Ron Cooke. As we noted in Chapter 4, it includes the requirement on institutions to publish various data about the quality of learning and teaching in order to give better information to potential students and their advisers, using the HERO portal. The institutional audit now includes judgements about the reliability of the institution's Cooke-related data and also its readiness to meet the requirements in making available the various information sets. This is all complemented by work to introduce a national system of gathering student feedback, the National Student Survey (NSS), designed to yield judgements about relative satisfaction at subject level between institutions. The NSS is now due to be conducted for the first time in full in 2005, drawing on responses from full- and part-time final year undergraduates. The intention is

> to help inform prospective students and their advisers, alongside other information on teaching quality, in making choices about what and where to study. It also aims to contribute to public accountability, and to provide information that will help institutions to enhance teaching quality, by supplementing internal feedback mechanisms.
>
> (HEFCE 2004d: 1)

Concerns remain about the cost of this approach and also, although the pilot was encouraging here, about the prospects of generating valid conclusions at a useful level of detail (see pages 147–149).

The NSS is intended to run alongside institutions' own efforts, and here too there has been encouraging national activity resulting in a good practice document for the LTSN (including a student feedback cycle) (Brennan and Williams 2004). The university adopted student feedback as the theme of its 2001–02 Annual Academic Health Process. Student feedback is routinely sought on all modules as well as through regular monitoring of individual services such as Information Services (library, learning resources, ICT). There are difficulties, however, in securing consistent student participation in course and School boards, despite efforts by the Students' Union to support representatives, and also in providing prompt feedback to students about any concerns raised. During 2004, the student written submission prepared by the University Students' Union for the institutional audit rated some aspects of provision particularly highly, including preparation for employment; value for money; levels of availability of library stock and accessibility of computing facilities;

the quality of the university's estate; high levels of awareness and praise for the student intranet in assisting learning. But it also raised some important concerns – about the timeliness of feedback on student work; accessibility of learning resources at all sites; consistency in marking and assessment of group work; and lack of confidence that submitting a written complaint would not impact negatively on future personal assessments (Appendix 1: University of Brighton Students' Union 2004). Work is now underway to address these concerns.

However, the national debate about the technicalities of publishing useful information and the possible costs of so doing threatens to obscure more important debate about the role of students in the quality process. Intelligent commentators recognize that there is a complex relationship between students and their university that cannot be reduced to regarding them merely as 'customers'. As Rob Cuthbert has observed, while the metaphor of 'customer care' can be useful, 'there are two kinds of problem: inadequate understanding of what "customer" means; and using the metaphor of "customer" in contexts where it is not helpful' (Cuthbert 2003: 1). He goes on to point out 'the several roles of the student' and concludes that 'it's important to get your ideas straight about whether students are members, learners, clients or customers. It's even more important to get your ideas straight about what it is they are members, learners, clients and customers for' (Cuthbert 2003: 7).

Notwithstanding these important considerations, the drive to connect student views with institutional reputation continues and we say more about this in Chapter 8.

Reporting on progress

The quality cycle brings together monitoring and reporting of progress at different levels of activity; reliable data about aspects of institutional performance; and external views from external examiners and professional and statutory bodies. Like the data and planning cycles, there is an annual process:

> The basic building block of the University's quality assurance system remains ... the maintenance of a strong and very well understood annual course and module monitoring framework undertaken as part of an annual academic health process.
>
> (Appendix 1 2004a: 47)

The **Annual Academic Health Process** is a thorough and far-reaching review of the academic year just gone, built up from course-level monitoring, accompanied by self-critical commentary on each year's particular theme. It culminates in two key outputs. The first is a comprehensive report to the Academic Board via the Academic Standards Committee that summarizes progress, issues and difficulties, and on which a judgement can be reached about the security of the university's awards. The second is a subsequent report to the **Academic Enhancement Day**. This event brings together senior staff across the university with academic and functional responsibilities to examine the outcomes of the Annual Academic Health Process and to agree those actions that need to be taken to address issues identified through the review. As such, it serves the purpose of both quality assurance and quality enhancement:

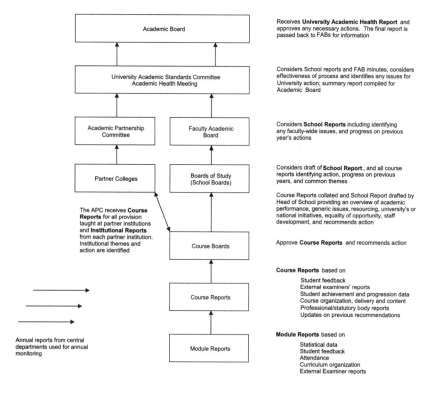

Figure 5.3 University of Brighton: the Academic Health Process
Source: Appendix 1 (2004a)

The Annual Academic Health Process is a major driver of quality enhancement for schools, faculties, central departments and the institution. The Annual Academic Health Report submitted to the Academic Board in Spring Term each year forms an axis for signing off action from the previous year and setting the agenda for the following year, including the thematic strand.

(University of Brighton 2004a: 38)

The purpose is to ensure that the university's academic provision is sound and that action is taken where it is found to be needed. Recent themes have included student retention, collecting and using student feedback and engagement with the QAA academic infrastructure. The Academic Health Process is illustrated in Figure 5.3.

At the end of the 2002–03 Academic Health Process, the conclusion was reached that there could be 'assurance both of the general academic health of the university's taught provision and of the engagement at all levels of the university in the processes of monitoring and evaluation' (Appendix 1 2003j: 8).

Table 5.3 University of Brighton: closing the quality loop

Concern	Action taken in response
About the fitness for purpose of parts of the university's estate, including timetabling; the pattern of rooms; local examples of noise pollution; and the need to improve integration of academic with estate planning	A summary of estate issues arising to be routinely considered by the University's Estates Committee; members of the Estates and Facilities Management Department joining Boards of Study and Faculty Academic Boards
About the university's relationship with partner colleges in the context of growing numbers of students on franchised courses	Establishing Partner College Review and the Academic Partnership Committee to systematically review quality assurance arrangements with college colleagues
That the Academic Health Process was disconnected from the implementation of the Learning and Teaching strategy	Individual examples of good practice identified during Academic Health should be formally collated and disseminated in the context of implementing the Learning and Teaching Strategy

Nonetheless, the process always throws up issues that need more attention. We noted above from the early institutional audits that institutions often find it difficult to 'close the loop'. Recognizing this, part of the university's **Enhancement Day** is charged with looking at the implementation of recommendations from the previous year, as well as making recommendations for further work. Often, these are about the potential and need for better connections to be made between different parts of the institution. Table 5.3 illustrates some recent examples.

In parallel to the Academic Health Process, the **Annual Academic Year Review** looks at regular qualitative and quantitative information and offers a focused and self-critical account of delivery by support departments. This has been discussed in Chapter 4.

Managing quality assurance is difficult in circumstances where legitimately produced self-criticism can be abused outside (by politicians, the media or your rivals), and when it can be cast inside as a distraction from core business. Institutional self-study confirms, however, that it is core business, and that, to be effective, it needs to be approached without fear.

6

THE PLANNING CYCLE

This book is about how institutions can improve their strategic planning and decision-making through self-study. This chapter explores how an institution can build an effective planning cycle suitably informed by self-study – in other words, how good self-study can help effective planning.

The planning framework

We noted in Chapter 2 reservations about the rational model of institutional planning, in which unambiguous and relevant information is readily available, easily interpreted, and can be used immediately in a straightforward way to assess uncertainty, develop strategic options and inform strategic decisions. Instead, we prefer to think more about institutional learning, and the 'learning school', well summarized by Mintzberg *et al.* (1998: 175–231) with both analytical and case study examples. They conclude: 'the learning school has served us well. Its research has been based on simple methods that seem well suited to explaining complex phenomena. But don't be fooled by the messiness of the process: this requires a great deal of sophistication' (Mintzberg *et al.* 1998: 230).

In this chapter, we describe one institution's attempts to establish good habits in its planning without excessive sophistication but with a commitment to improvement. For the University of Brighton, the purpose of the planning cycle is to enable it to develop and maintain plans that take it forward in the light both of its institutional history and of its mission, and to take well-informed strategic decisions, particularly about its teaching, research and 'third stream' activities. As with the data and quality cycles, there are internal and external audiences who sometimes have different interests. In this, we hope to avoid the 'unsafe refuge' or 'false panacea' eloquently described by Duke, *apropos* managing in Australian higher education (Duke 2002: 6).

The resulting planning framework is expressed in the 2004 Self-evaluation Document (SED) as follows. It is designed to:

- equip the university to identify and articulate strategic priorities that reflect its intellectual and institutional inheritance, respond to external drivers, and are ambitious but attainable;
- identify specific targets to be achieved and, as a basis for monitoring progress against them, related to clearly identified responsibility for delivery;
- involve as many staff as possible;
- offer a distinctive 'Brighton' position on major issues of policy and practice;
- inform local decision-making and resource allocation; and
- provide a platform for collaborative working.

(Appendix 1 2004a)

This requires a framework and layers of activity, something that is strongly iterative, rather than a sequential process or single all-encompassing (and probably unusable) document. Consequently, the planning framework has a number of elements:

- the Corporate Plan 2002–07, finalized following extensive consultation internally and externally;
- faculty and department strategic plans developed in the first half of 2003, followed up by meetings on resource aspects between Deans and senior colleagues (summer 2003), and on student number aspirations between the Strategic Planning Unit and Faculty Management Groups (autumn 2003);
- a series of thematic strategies covering priorities in research, learning and teaching, widening participation, staffing, commercialization, marketing and finance;
- ongoing reflection of planning issues on a subject or disciplinary basis, and their implications for the university's portfolio and how it is organized;
- an annual operating statement specifying the top 30 or so institution-wide priorities for the year to come;
- annual agreement about student number targets by course, school and faculty for each source of funding (and including targets for partner college provision); and

- regular reflective monitoring of progress, against a schedule described in the Corporate Plan.

Table 6.1 illustrates the totality of this planning framework, indicating the horizon, scope and authority for each element, or planning statement, who agrees them and who evaluates progress, as well as the external audience (where applicable).

The planning cycle   ■

The number of elements in the planning framework and their differential scope can make creating anything coherent from them quite challenging. Add to this the necessity – recommended in any self-respecting guidance on good planning – to include both the 'top down' and the 'bottom up', as well as the common university desire to include the 'inside out' and the 'outside in', and the mix is indeed demanding. As with data and quality, we argue that planning is best assisted by a straightforward annual cycle, in which self-study supports effective planning in two main ways, first in helping inform the content of the plan and secondly in encouraging a self-critical approach to evaluating progress against the plan.

Bringing together the analysis so far suggests a number of characteristics of an effective planning cycle. Some of these are common to the data and quality cycles and include:

- a design which reflects the specific values and aspirations of the individual institution;
- careful integration with other institutional activity, especially the planning and quality cycles and the committee or business cycles; and with clear assignment of roles and responsibilities;
- a transparent, intelligent and self-critical approach to gathering the necessary evidence and to monitoring progress;
- good organization and management, with the ability to meet internal and external requirements through understanding the priorities (as well as the blind-spots) of the various stakeholders;
- engagement across the institution, ensuring coverage of all the relevant activities and issues and involvement of those with different expertise and responsibilities;
- support for risk management; and
- provision of a framework for strategic decision-making and evaluation.

Table 6.1 University of Brighton: the planning framework

Planning statement	Horizon	Scope	Agreed by	Progress evaluated by	External audience
Corporate Plan	5 years (current plan covers 2002–07)	University – all strategic issues	Board of Governors, advised by Academic Board	Board of Governors	HEFCE; Annual Report
Strategic plans	5 years	Faculties and departments – strategic issues facing authoring unit	Faculty Management Groups; functional committees	Faculty Management Groups; functional committees	
Operating statement	1 year	University – top 30 or so targets that must be achieved in year if Corporate Plan overall is to be achieved	Board of Governors, advised by Academic Board and Management Group	Board of Governors, advised by Academic Board and Management Group	HEFCE
Thematic strategies	Varies but mostly 5 years	University – for individual themes (e.g. widening participation; research; commercial; staffing)	Varies but mainly Academic Board or functional committee including committees of the Board of Governors	Progress against major strategies is reviewed by responsible committee of the Board of Governors or Academic Board	HEFCE (in some cases)
Subject analysis	Ongoing	University – subjects or disciplines	Academic Board	Academic Board	
Student number targets	1 year, with indicative targets for 3 years	Course, level, mode, funding source; aggregated into Schools, faculties and sites	Management Group	Management Group, Academic Development Committee, Academic Board, Board of Governors (contract compliance)	Funding body contracts (HEFCE, TTA, NHS)

In addition, there are some characteristics specific to the planning cycle:

- respect for institutional history (see Figure 6.2);
- providing a basis for institution to engage with the external environment;
- enabling the institution to deal with events for which it has not planned;
- realism about both the need for and the pace of change – 'an appropriate balance of continuity and change' (Appendix 1 2003a: 3);
- critical engagement with and responsiveness to external policy developments.

The planning cycle at Brighton is iterative rather than sequential. It is not the case that one cycle works towards a complete set of planning statements and that the institution then starts again. Rather, there is a dynamic relationship between the elements of the planning framework described above, in which they inform each other, and in which progress informs both a view about the adequacy of the current statement and the preparation of future statements.

This is shown in Figure 6.1: faculty and department strategic plans are informed by the Corporate Plan and the thematic strategies and also inform, through their content and a review of progress against them, both the next Corporate Plan and an understanding of the continued 'fit' of the current Corporate Plan.

Of the characteristics of an effective planning cycle, **historical sense** is one of the most important. It provides a context for decisions some of which will emphasize continuity, while others seek to restore historical commitments, and others will aim at significant change. For example, Figure 6.2 sets out how the University of the West of England visualized itself at the moment of university designation.

The introduction to the University of Brighton's Corporate Plan attempts to capture the same sense of pride and challenge:

> Brighton is the product of a succession of creative alliances of initially separate foundations ... This plan for the next five years reflects an appropriate balance of continuity and change. It reinforces commitments to professional formation and to civic engagement. It seeks to meet new challenges, especially of lifelong learning, of social inclusion, and of knowledge exchange in an information-rich age.
>
> (Appendix 1 2003a: 3)

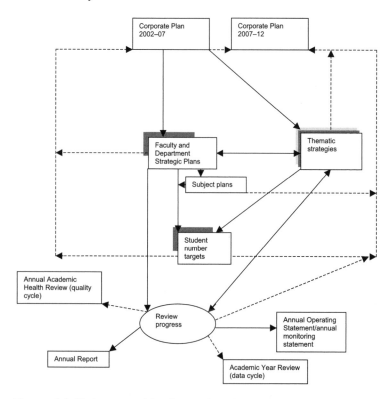

Figure 6.1 University of Brighton: the planning cycle

Engaging with the external environment is also vital. At first sight, **environmental scanning** would appear to be outside the scope of self-study since by definition it is about looking outside the institution. However, as we commented in Chapter 3, self-study is in part about strategic scoping – supporting strategic choices – and therefore about understanding the external environment. We consider the wider political issues in Chapter 7.

Figure 6.3 illustrates some of the ways in which the external environment was brought into play in the part of the planning cycle that generated the university's Corporate Plan for 2002–07. It indicates an explicit place for environmental scanning to help in assessing the continued relevance of the previous plan; external consultation (which involved circulating some 300 individuals and organizations); and creating a number of scenarios for consideration by the Board (which were also made available on the intranet for staff). It is worthy of note that the university's previous plan covered

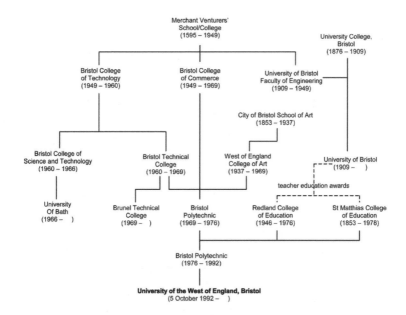

Figure 6.2 University of the West of England: history
Source: University of the West of England

the period 1999–2004 but that the current plan addresses 2002–07. The ongoing assessment of relevance indicated strongly to the Board and others by mid–2001 that a revised plan would be required before the notional end of the life of the then current plan, because of its decreasingly adequate fit with external and internal circumstances and imperatives. This early return to medium-term plans is not uncommon in large private as well as public sector organizations.

External consultation was conducted by means of a personal letter from the Vice-Chancellor to about 300 individuals and organizations with whom the university worked or whose opinion it particularly valued. The letter included a consultation paper offering a provisional assessment of progress against the then current plan and identifying some of the major issues facing the institution, with some specific questions. Internal consultation, in some ways a different form of scanning, also included a personal letter from the Vice-Chancellor and the discussion and question paper, complemented in this case by a series of open meetings at each of the university's sites. An analysis of the responses was considered by the Academic Board and Board of Governors early in 2002.

One of the ways of bringing the external environment up-front in

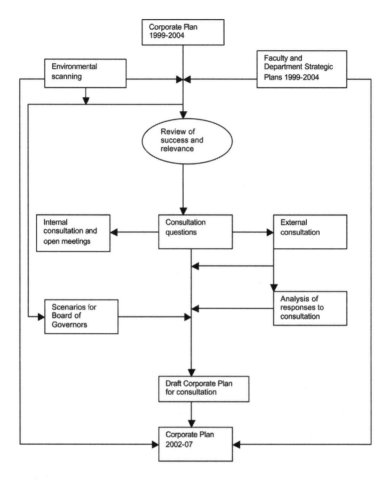

Figure 6.3 University of Brighton: environmental scanning and the corporate plan

the planning cycle is to build a small number of scenarios and consider their possible implications for the institution. The purpose of **scenario-building** is not to make predictions but rather to enable the institution to cope better with whatever the future unfolds, by stimulating 'more innovative options' (Schoemaker 1995: 205). 'When the organization has established a broad base of strategic intelligence and has a continuous scanning and monitoring system, scenario planning works well' (Liston 1999: 76). Some private sector organizations have built scenarios for a number of years as part of their planning processes and the practice is becoming more popular in the public sector, partly as a response to growing sensitivities to risk and partly following active government promotion (Cabinet Office 2001a, 2001b, 2001c). There are interesting examples of the technique from the Economic and Social Research Council (ESRC)/Office of Science and Technology (OST) and the European Commission that make useful reference points for institutional strategic planning (ESRC/OST 1999; European Commission 1999).

There is arguably a 'hard' and a 'soft' side to scenario building (although these are not mutually exclusive). The harder side recommends formal tools and testing, most simply through the technique of identifying factors that will affect the future and concentrating effort on those that are less likely to be part of daily management, as well as high in uncertainty, impact and importance, since by definition these are more likely, if they become real, to have a greater impact. This leads to the following typology:

- highly uncertain and high impact/importance;
- low uncertainty and high impact/importance;
- highly uncertain and low impact/importance;
- low uncertainty and low impact/importance.

(Adapted from O'Brien 2002)

The softer side regards this activity as a high-quality 'strategic conversation' (van der Heijden 1996: xiii) and 'a social process, individuals working together to combine their spontaneous insights as a way to scaffold each other's tacit knowledge that is as yet unconnected' (van der Heijden 1997: 8).

The University made its first forays into scenario building as part of the early preparations for its 2002–07 Corporate Plan, in a Board of Governors' seminar, accompanied by contributions from a small number of its own academics with informed perspectives on particular issues. The intention was, at the softer end of the spectrum, to offer some conversational stimuli and to be provocative. It was also explicitly connected with a parallel exercise by the local authority, because of the University's perception that its fortunes are implicated in those of the local area – and how it is perceived objectively and subjectively (Brighton and Hove City Council 1999). Three scenarios were developed: 'renaissance', 'second cold war' and 'e-barony', as shown in Table 6.2.

Table 6.2 University of Brighton: summary of scenarios for 2010

'renaissance' – a future in which the City of Brighton and Hove and those who live and work in it are generally prosperous, HE participation is above current levels, but the nature of academic work and student learning is dramatically different. HE is deeply internationally engaged
'second cold war' – a future in which the local economy is stagnant; HE student debt has increased and the costs to students are differentiated by region of study. HEIs are more local in their focus and students more instrumental in their choices
'e-barony' – a future in which the city and HE are increasingly polarized; fees are differentiated by subject and institution; the sector has been restructured

The planning pack

Continuing with the question of content in the planning cycle, the most general and wide-ranging contribution to the planning cycle is via the planning pack. This is a loose-leaf folder given to each Dean, Head and member of the senior management team intended to aid them in their planning efforts, and to provoke thinking about strategic issues. It contains a diverse set of information, periodically updated (with ten instalments between its instigation in December 2000 and summer 2004). Alongside a copy of the university's planning framework, example contents include:

- data on enrolments and applications;
- material, including newspaper articles, about the university's locality;
- information on supply and demand for higher education;
- information on broader social change relevant to higher education;
- key policy statements, for example speeches from ministers;
- advice on planning techniques including scenarios and other 'futures' work;
- copies of HEFCE's strategic plan and letter of grant;
- the university's responses to key documents such as the 2003 White Paper;
- university policies (for example on equalities) and the thematic strategies (including research, widening participation, staffing, learning and teaching, and commercial).

The planning pack is not expected to appeal in every item to every recipient, to be put to immediate use, or to replace subject-based or subject-specific information in which colleagues are expert. Rather, its purpose is to support a culture of awareness and reflection, as well as to provide a single point of reference for some key documents about the sector and the University's policy stance. It sits alongside the reports on quantitative data described in Chapter 4. Over time, more use has been made of the university's intranet to locate and cross-reference internally produced information, particularly information with a dynamic nature, such as the data on applications also described in that chapter.

Planning for teaching and learning

As indicated in Figure 6.4, the University plans its student numbers annually within the context of: the overall targets in its Corporate Plan; faculty five-yearly strategic plans; medium-term plans for the academic portfolio across the institution; resource issues; implications of relevant thematic strategies; and trends in applications and enrolments. This part of the planning cycle aims to secure a balance between the imperatives of student demand, external policy and funding 'pushes' on the one hand, and an academic shape that makes sense to the university on the other. This can be complex – and sometimes frustrating: it needs to take account of the 'terms of trade' offered by the funding bodies, including those by which additional public funding might be available for additional provision, constraints of accommodation and staffing, the possible speed of change, the relationship between teaching and research. For Brighton, it also has to take account of the aspirations of partner colleges (and other universities with which we have specific areas of collaboration) and the views of professional and statutory bodies. It also takes place with distinctly imperfect information – particularly about the behaviour of other institutions and, of course, the intentions of potential applicants. There is therefore a strong element of 'risk', and much of the planning cycle is designed to try to minimize the exposure to, and possible impact of, that risk. In this, the planning cycle is strongly intertwined with the data cycle; for example, the work on market intelligence described in Chapter 4 is at the heart of institutional planning for teaching and learning.

Minimizing these risks in an intelligent way matters, because getting the right shape overall not only determines the amount of teaching and fee income flowing into the university and its unit of funding but also significantly influences internal resource allocations, patterns of staffing and accommodation plans, and the scope for new development or investments. Getting this significantly wrong can quite quickly lead to crisis. The planning cycle for setting student number targets is illustrated in Figure 6.4.

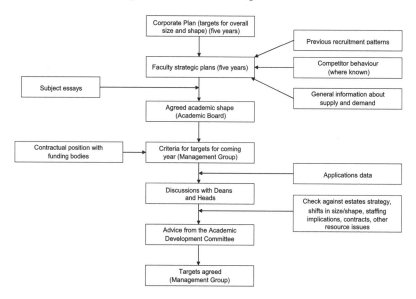

Figure 6.4 University of Brighton: setting student number targets

It takes several meetings – informal as well as formal – to drive this process. Targets are confirmed by the Management Group, following agreement at the start of the annual planning round about the criteria to be adopted and detailed negotiations with individual Deans and Heads of School. There are a number of iterations to ensure that the overall picture makes sense for the institution as a whole, the demands on its different sites, shifts in student demand, and the overall contractual position – as well as that it is realistic. Targets are agreed for each year of each course, and also by mode and funding source, although of course in practice what matters are broad numbers in each School or cognate groups of courses within a School. To date, it has tended to be relatively collegial (partly because of institutional culture and partly because of a climate of overall growth), although there are of course alternative models (see Shattock 2003a: 63, on 'constructive confrontation').

For 2004–05, the 'decision rules' agreed to guide target-setting were as set out below:

- that the University would not wish to grow significantly overall if this involves diminishing the HEFCE unit of resource for teaching;
- that courses which have not recruited well in more than one recent year and in which applications are problematic, and/or in which significant numbers enter through Clearing, should be considered for reductions in targets, if there is no convincing 'recovery plan' and if this is consistent with overall academic shape. A decision may be needed in some cases about minimum levels for viability;
- that unfettered growth should not be supported for courses that have recruited exceptionally strongly if this implies immediate and significant new staffing or other resource requirements;
- that judgements are required about the realism of those Schools planning significant changes in emphasis between undergraduate and postgraduate taught provision where this relies on decisions by individuals within the local labour market;
- that research numbers should continue to be targeted for growth wherever this is consistent with research plans and resources;
- that Schools should aim for first year cohorts of at least 100 full-time undergraduates in order to be viable; and
- that international student numbers should continue to be targeted for growth even if this takes the University further above the Corporate Plan indicator of success.

Nationally, some curious things seemed to be going on as the university undertook this exercise. As we saw in Chapter 4, trends in the number of institutions offering provision in some subject areas run counter to the number of students studying those subjects. Similarly, recent national data show that the number of students enrolling on engineering courses exceeds the number applying to do so (Sterling 2002). We also have the sustained phenomenon of students making rational choices which their elders despise, whether of institutions (for example choosing locality over others' perception of prestige) or of subjects (like media) (Watson 2003b).

Locally, there have inevitably been 'hits' and 'misses' – renaming or repositioning groups of courses that has led to a dramatic and unanticipated decrease in applications; a new medical school (jointly with the University of Sussex) that saw the highest application rate of the group in its second year; a new course for the digital TV industry designed and supported by them but launched just at the point of sector economic downturn, to take just three examples. What we seem to have is a correlation between academic development – a consistent flow of well thought out and intellectually grounded new 'products' – and the ability to increase the number and/or calibre of applicants and enrolments. The management implications of this, particularly the use of creative cross-subsidy, are discussed in more detail in Chapter 7.

Considerations for the right academic portfolio include the pattern of awards to be offered and where subjects should best be located structurally within the university to give them academic dynamism yet necessary stability. For example, on the pattern of awards, should the University offer professional doctorates (yes); should it withdraw from civil engineering (no); should it embrace foundation degrees (yes, but rather reluctantly given its success with HNDs and the lack of evidence of strong demand for the new qualification)? On academic organization, ongoing debates include how to optimize work on aspects of media that have proper academic 'homes' in at least six Schools on four different sites; aspects of design and production in which those from disciplines as disparate as fine art and engineering have an interest; how to deliver interprofessional education to professions including doctors, pharmacists, physiotherapists, podiatrists, nurses and midwives.

As background to these debates, Table 3.1 (on pages 27–30) sets out the University's Corporate Plan objectives for its size and shape.

Planning for research ∎

HEIs need a research strategy because 'the nature of the higher education enterprise is inescapably research-related' (Appendix 1 2003a: 8) and because they need to find a way of relating their research activity to their overall academic shape.

Bushaway, in a detailed account in this series, argues that institutions need to articulate what they do in research: in relation to the external policy and funding context; to comply with legislation; to fit personal plans with corporate aspirations; and because 'successful research strategies tend to lead to more successful research' (Bushaway 2003: 37). To this, we would argue, should be added the need to understand and promote the relationship between research and teaching, and also between research and 'third stream' activity. Bushaway also argues that a research strategy is dependent on good analysis, preferably including a SWOT (strengths, weaknesses, opportunities, threats); good understanding of costs in order to be able to take pricing decisions; the ability to measure time usage meaningfully; a map of funding opportunities; market understanding; and personal plans for researchers. This careful approach underlines the importance of extensive and honest self-knowledge that takes time and care to assemble and to keep 'live'.

It is an approach in which the institution is also a customer of research: 'the University aims to use the findings of research in its own development and in all of its operating practices. It is committed to the adoption of evidence-based practice in its current activities and in future changes and developments' (Appendix 1 2004f: 1.6). It also implies coordinated effort across a number of functions of the university – finance, personnel, public relations, schools and faculties or research units.

Bushaway's survey makes clear that the picture is further complicated by the range of activities to be understood; from the needs of research students to the rules of the different research councils and charitable trusts; from the requirements of the Patent Office to the need to nurture individuals across many different subjects; from the understanding of research ethics in different disciplines to knowledge of complex EU funding regulations. He writes largely from a 'big science' and research-intensive background, but he offers a valuable reminder that research doesn't just happen – it needs to be managed well: 'research requires development as a continuous process measured against new challenges and stated objectives which should be set, reviewed, renewed and resourced in a given period of time' (Bushaway 2003: 192).

Like many other institutions, the University of Brighton has revisited its research strategy following the outcomes of the 2001 RAE and the subsequent national review of research selectivity, the 2003 White Paper and the Lambert Review for HM Treasury (HMT) (DfES 2003; HMT 2003). That strategy is not, perhaps surprisingly, geared to success in the next RAE, but also to continuing to build the capacity for high-quality research rather than short-term positioning. While the University has been successful through successive RAEs in comparison with other 'new' universities, its chief concern is to use the resulting formula funding (QR, or quality-based research funding) to 'gear' other sources of support. Table 6.3 shows its position in the HEFCE league table of research funding (incidentally, the only league table which continues to separate all new from all old universities, as the goalposts for post-RAE funding have been moved). Table 6.4 shows the sources of geared income, which now leaves 'R' funding from the funding council as less than 40 per cent of the University's research-related income.

In these circumstances, the intention is 'to ensure that a substantial critical mass of research activity exists and continues to be developed and enhanced in all the major subject areas in which [the University] currently offers taught provision'; to increase the amount of research income by 50 per cent over seven years; to increase the number of research students; and to enhance the research infrastructure (Appendix 1 2004f). This is in the context where 'the

Table 6.3 HEFCE: 'R' funding as a percentage of 'T' + 'R', 2004–05

Rank	Institution	% Funding via research
1	Imperial College of Science, Technology and Medicine	58.0%
2	University of Cambridge	57.7%
3	University of Oxford	57.6%
4	University College London	57.6%
5	University of York	45.2%
6	University of Southampton	44.0%
7	University of Manchester Institute of Science & Technology	42.6%
8	University of Surrey	42.5%
9	University of Manchester	40.9%
10	Royal Holloway, University of London	40.6%
11	King's College London	40.5%
12	University of Reading	39.8%
13	University of Sheffield	39.3%
14	University of Warwick	39.1%
15	University of Bristol	37.7%
16	University of Sussex	36.3%
17	University of East Anglia	35.0%
18	University of Bath	34.7%
19	University of Nottingham	33.9%
20	Lancaster University	33.9%
21	University of Newcastle upon Tyne	33.9%
22	University of Birmingham	33.8%
23	University of Durham	32.0%
24	University of Leeds	31.3%
25	Goldsmiths College, University of London	30.5%
26	University of Essex	30.5%
27	University of Leicester	30.4%
28	University of Liverpool	28.9%
29	University of Exeter	26.4%
30	Birkbeck College	26.0%
31	Loughborough University	25.6%
32	Queen Mary, University of London	24.1%
33	Aston University	22.7%
34	Keele University	22.0%
35	City University, London	19.8%
36	University of Bradford	19.3%
37	Brunel University	17.1%
38	University of Kent	14.9%
39	University of Hull	13.4%
40	University of Salford	12.7%
41	University of Brighton	9.1%

42	University of Portsmouth	8.0%
43	De Montfort University	6.7%
44	Oxford Brookes University	5.9%
45	University of Surrey Roehampton	5.8%
46	Sheffield Hallam University	4.8%
47	Nottingham Trent University	4.7%
48	Liverpool John Moores University	4.6%
49	University of Hertfordshire	4.5%
50	University of Plymouth	4.1%
51	Manchester Metropolitan University	3.8%
52	Open University	3.7%
53	University of East London	3.7%
54	University of Gloucestershire	3.7%
55	London South Bank University	3.6%
56	Middlesex University	3.6%
57	University of Westminster	3.3%
58	University of the West of England, Bristol	3.3%
59	University of Huddersfield	3.3%
60	University of Greenwich	2.7%
61	University of Sunderland	2.3%
62	University of Luton	2.1%
63	Coventry University	2.0%
64	Kingston University	2.0%
65	Bournemouth University	1.8%
66	University of Northumbria at Newcastle	1.8%
67	University of Central Lancashire	1.8%
68	University of Central England in Birmingham	1.4%
69	Leeds Metropolitan University	1.4%
70	Staffordshire University	1.4%
71	Anglia Polytechnic University	1.4%
72	University of Teesside	1.2%
73	University of Derby	1.0%
74	University of Wolverhampton	1.0%
75	London Metropolitan University	0.8%
76	University of Lincoln	0.7%
77	Thames Valley University	0.2%

Source: Based on HEFCE (2004b)

University of Brighton is characterised as much by its research as its teaching, and the two activities can and should wherever possible inform and revitalise each other', and where research activity, while diverse, 'is distinguished, at least in part, by its applicability either to specific economic or social transformation or to professional or creative practice' (Appendix 1 2004f: 1.3 and 1.5).

The purpose of self-study in this context is threefold:

Table 6.4 University of Brighton: sources of research income, 2003–04

	£000	%
Research Councils	1,599	19.0%
UK-based charities	106	1.3%
UK central and local government, health authorities	1,128	13.4%
UK industry and commerce	609	7.3%
EU government bodies	648	7.7%
EU other	107	1.3%
Other overseas research	87	1.0%
Sub-total	**4,284**	
Knowledge transfer partnerships (TCS)	802	9.5%
Sub-total	**5,086**	**60.5%**
HEFCE 'R' Funds (QR etc.)	3,314	39.5%
Total all sources	**8,400**	**100%**

- to make sure that research plans are soundly based given the strengths of the individual researchers, the developments in the field, the priorities of funding bodies, likely peer judgements, and the relationship between the local research plan and the overall institutional strategy;
- to support resource decisions, both the overall support for research in which the institution chooses to invest or can afford, and between research groups and possibly individuals. These decisions, whether about money, equipment, buildings or people and how they are able to use their time, must be well-informed, transparent, and supportive of the overall strategy. This means that they need to fit at an individual level, and that approaches will differ across the sector: Shattock, for example, describes the harder-edged approach of the University of Warwick to areas not scoring sufficiently highly in the RAE (Shattock 2003a: 164). Some institutions routinely employ external mentors or leading academics to help them reach judgements of merit and potential, since it is intrinsically so difficult to get this right by internal judgements alone. In most institutions, these decisions will aim to balance support to sustain established groups with support for those that might achieve excellence given investment (and perhaps good fortune).

In many institutions, whether 'research intensive' or not, this is still 'work in progress', particularly where efforts continue to master what might pass for a full understanding of research costs (accentuated by the drive towards Full Economic Costing); and
- to enable the institution to evaluate progress towards achieving its research aspirations.

As recommended by Bushaway's guide, the operational arm of Brighton's research strategy requires detailed local research plans, prepared by groups, Schools and Faculties that set minimum goals and aspirational targets, with annual monitoring. These plans need to relate to the thematic research strategy (an iterative relationship indicated in Figure 6.1). They are expected to relate to the 'particular requirements of subject areas and the existing research base' [and] 'be clearly identifiable as a subset of the overall academic plan for the School/Faculty' (Appendix 1 2004f). They are expected to include targets, covering the number and proportion of research active staff, through specific outputs, to indicators of esteem. Support departments are also expected to refer to research when setting their own plans, for example when planning estates developments or determining priorities for investment in networks or libraries.

Delivering these sorts of plans in an effective way suggests that self-study to support research planning must consist in large part of knowing the individuals and teams that are actively engaged, their strengths and weaknesses, interests and potential, since it is the individuals, not the institution, that do the research (Bushaway 2003: 193). This requires a sensible and sensitive structure within academic departments that can combine ambition with realism; support an honest assessment of what is possible; and engage critically with developments in the research discipline nationally and internationally as well as with the institution's policies and practices. Again, both knowledge of the internal and external context is necessary. This knowledge needs to be assembled close to the individuals and teams doing the research because aspects of it will be highly specific. Good research leadership is therefore essential. But it also needs to be part of an institutional system with some central coordination, leadership, organizational support, management and metrics, in order to inform and be informed by the institution's overall research capacity and direction.

Planning for business and community engagement ▮

Most if not all HEIs have institutional objectives that involve increasing their income from sources other than teaching and research and reducing their dependence on funding council income. For some, such plans concentrate on a relatively narrow income-related dimension of activity that is based on the development of commercial spin-offs from mainstream teaching and research. For others, there will be a wider, more differentiated and subtler package of work that includes not only primarily commercial undertakings but also engagement with local communities, which might have a very different financial basis. Commercial and community engagement – conventionally referred to in the UK as 'third stream activity' – can therefore be highly diffuse and diverse both within and between institutions. This makes it harder to conceptualize and articulate clearly, let alone to evaluate. In turn, this makes the related self-study challenge more problematic.

Much of the attention until recently, in the UK at least, has been on trying to describe and measure the impact of higher education institutions on their local economies, in the context of attempts to articulate better the overall economic and social contribution to the UK economy of the higher education sector. In part, this is a result of the pressure to justify public investment in higher education. During the early 1990s a number of individual institutions embarked on studies of their own impact. This was given impetus both by the conceptual and technical frameworks developed by the Goddard team at the University of Newcastle and the McNicoll team at the University of Strathclyde (Goddard *et al.* 1994; McNicoll *et al.* 1997), as well as by the implicit endorsement of such approaches in the Dearing Report. Dearing commissioned research into 'higher education and the regions' and devoted a chapter to 'those aspects of higher education to which locality and proximity are important', arguing that 'there is much to be gained by fostering the active engagement of institutions with localities and regions' (NCIHE 1997: 189 and 191; Robson *et al.* 1997).

Most recently, the 2003 White Paper and the Lambert Report have talked up the importance of 'third stream' activity, identified some of the ways in which it can work well, and brought to the fore discussions about how best to fund and foster it, following some early and arguably tentative forays by HEFCE through HEROBAC (Higher Education Reach-out to Business and the Community) and HEIF (Higher Education Innovation Fund) (DfES 2003; HMT 2003). UUK has added to the debate through its work on evaluating the overall contribution of the sector (UUK 2001b; Kelly *et al.* 2002).

The challenges here for the planning cycle are threefold, and similar to those applicable to research and teaching. The planning cycle needs to help ensure that:

- planning for 'third stream' work is soundly based, in the light of the underpinning activity of teaching and research, overall institutional capacity and external opportunities and needs. Typically, this will need some sort of brokerage or boundary-spanning role, at least in relation to traditional university activity, and there are likely to be some particular challenges of knowledge management for the individuals in such roles and relationship management for the institution as a whole. It will also require judgements about risk, resource investment and the pace of change;
- 'third stream' work is suitably reflective in scope and definition of the underlying institutional values and priorities; and
- the activity can be evaluated, with identified targets and assessments of progress, impact and effectiveness, particularly if the scope of the activity is larger than income generation and/or has a 'softer' focus.

Some of this looks familiar – what is the right portfolio; how can we ensure a good understanding of costing and pricing; how can we understand funding opportunities; how can we engage individuals and help to manage the overall time resources of teams, Schools and others; how do we prioritize between activities; how do we best organize central functions to deliver critical support to Schools who are delivering the work; how do we know that what we are doing is working? Similarly, like research, this requires quite detailed knowledge of what is going on that can only be assembled by people working closely with each other, as well as the capacity to spot the potential for links between areas that may currently not be working together, or between the institution's expertise and emerging external requirements and opportunities.

To these we need to add a vital prior consideration – about values and priorities, and a vital practical consideration: the 'third stream', whatever its particular scope within an individual institution, only operates in relationship to teaching and research expertise and interests. The trick is therefore to find some solutions in the planning cycle that can maximize that relationship to benefit more than one of the 'streams' simultaneously.

A recent analysis, based in part on extensive responses from international senior academics, generates a valuable picture of current UK perception and practice and should help HEIs to clarify their individual answer to the question of scope and definition (Slowey

2003). Slowey depicts higher education and its external communities as connected by a triangle involving the three partners of the state, the private sector and civil society (Slowey 2003: 139). The nature of engagement is categorized in a fourfold typology, depending on what the author describes as the breadth or orientation and on the primary emphasis:

- 'knowledge transfer' – broad orientation, economic emphasis;
- 'default' – focused orientation and economic emphasis, encompassing anything that is not teaching or research;
- widening participation – focused orientation and social emphasis, looking largely at individual participation;
- 'civil and community' – broad orientation and social focus, looking at engagement with public and civil society.

(Slowey 2003: 141)

Slowey argues that the policy preoccupation with commercial activity and income generation – concentration on the knowledge transfer mode – is played out in England in the HEFCE proposals for benchmarking an institution's engagement in its region, which concentrate six of the seven indicators on measuring economic impact.

At the University of Brighton, the Corporate Plan reflects the spectrum that Slowey identifies. Hence, there are commitments both to 'nurture its intellectual capital ethically, imaginatively and sustainably, and make this widely available' and also to 'collaborate actively with selected local, regional, national and international partners on the basis of mutual respect' (Appendix 1 2003a: 4). Specific objectives and indicators of success include:

- implementing a commercial strategy 'that secures the successful exploitation of and community gain from research, development, innovation and knowledge transfer, and that sustains the long-term impact of initiative funding after the initial funding period' and that will increase the income from third stream activities by 7 per cent compound growth (Appendix 1 2003a: 9);
- increasing the number of volunteering opportunities for students and making sure this can be recognized within their degrees;
- identifying and implementing ways of fostering student and staff enterprise initiatives;
- developing further the partnerships and frameworks necessary for effective exploitation of research and development;
- opening a business and innovation centre; and

- further development of alternative sources of income and reduction of dependence on public funds.

The commercial strategy approved by the Board of Governors, which is therefore only a part of the whole 'third stream' endeavour, notes that

> in developing the commercial strategy we must not forget that the resulting activities will be delivered by the same staff who are responsible for teaching and research within the institution. The detailed implementation of the strategy seeks to integrate these three activities rather than see them as competitive.
>
> (Appendix 1 2003c).

It further identifies the purpose of the commercial strategy as:

- developing core funding to support the overall mission;
- securing substantial educational benefits through enhancing the experience of staff and students; and
- becoming an integral part of the university.

There are several sources of advice available to assist in evaluating 'third stream' work. The most obvious is the annual survey carried out by HEFCE that concentrates on the commercially oriented end of the spectrum. The higher education–business interaction (HE–BI) survey 'incorporates both numerical metrics ... and objective qualitative indicators' (HEFCE 2004a: 1). As well as the discipline of completing the survey and the information gained directly from so doing, institutions are able to compare their own performance against the sector on a number of dimensions that touch on both the process of 'third stream' planning and the outcomes. Examples range from 'softer' information about the quality of relevant partnerships, through sector practice on staff incentives and intellectual property, to 'harder' financial indicators of income earned and the value of contracts.

Work led by the University of Salford offers a useful approach to trying to evaluate the impact of activity that goes beyond the conventional knowledge transfer paradigm. The Salford team has designed a framework that should enable some benchmarking (and they have identified a number of pairs of institutions willing to try). The framework involves four themes – business capital, social capital, individual capital and academic capital. The idea is to find 'some of the ways in which we can begin to think about the key characteristics of any successful university–business–community collaboration, and with possible indicators and metrics relating to these characteristics' (Salford University, see web reference [www.upbeat.org.uk]). To this can be added work commissioned by the Association of Commonwealth Universities to develop a benchmarking or self-assessment tool to enable institutions to assess their 'engagement' (Watson 2004). This follows the ACU's important work on 'the imperative of engagement', defined as

> strenuous, thoughtful, argumentative interaction with the non-university world in at least four spheres: setting universities' aims, purposes and priorities; relating teaching and learning to the wider world; the back-and-forth dialogue between researchers and practitioners; and taking on wider responsibilities as neighbours and citizens,

together with a simple checklist 'that institutional leaders might ask in order to gauge the institution's level and location of engagement' (ACU 2001: 1, i and 41–3).

In addition to the HE–BI survey, HEFCE has produced a benchmarking tool to support self-assessment of an institution's regional contribution, growing out of the Newcastle and Strathclyde Universities work described earlier (HEFCE 2002c). This is intended to enable assessment of improvements in individual regional engagement as well as to support collaborative strategies by institutions within a region. Even if an institution chooses not to adopt the full benchmarking model, which would be a demanding undertaking, the framework that informs the tool is valuable in highlighting relevant 'self-study' questions across a spectrum that includes 'redistributive processes', 'social capital development processes' as well as 'business development processes', and that includes some basic pointers to good practice (HEFCE 2002c: 10). More recently, HEFCE has instituted work to examine possible metrics for this sort of 'third stream' activity as it searches for a formulaic allocation methodology.

Planning for staff and resources

Much of the account here is concerned directly or indirectly with securing resources for the institution and with their internal distribution. The data, quality and planning cycles should help institutions to do this transparently and in support of institutional objectives, as well as to keep track of the flows of resource and their utilization. One of the particular benefits of the planning cycle should be that it assists in making sense of the various streams of income and enables the institution to take a strategic view of these. This should include the mix of formula and bid funds operated by HEFCE, which run alongside mainstream teaching and research funds. The mix includes those in support of staffing strategies, estates and infrastructure development, widening participation and retention, additional student numbers, learning and teaching strategies and third stream activity. Two tricks are necessary for institutional sanity here. The first is to be able to meet the information requirements of the funding bodies (since even if institutions don't have to bid they usually have to write an 'essay' to unlock the funds set aside for them). The second is to get the best possible – and honest – match between the funder's rubric and the institution's own priorities. HEFCE believes that it helps here by increasingly inviting institutions to show how their bid, or 'essay', fits with their strategic plan. However, in practice it does not feel as if this approach really enables that fit to be achieved, or indeed saves institutional effort, although it may be relocating the latter within the institution, since it remains the case that some of this work may go beyond or differ in form from that which institutions would do for themselves (PA Consulting 2004b).

Here, once more, external advice is plentiful, although again its utility is variable. Useful examples include the independently commissioned work for HEFCE on HR strategies by the Office for Public Management (OPM), which goes to the heart of achieving a strategic view of staffing capacity and needs alongside straightforward good personnel practice. It also notes how much further institutions need to go. Weaknesses include lack of basic information about the staff population and personnel processes: 'it is evident that, for many, the vision of the modern, integrated approach to strategic HR is not yet fully embedded' (OPM 2002: 37).

There is also a range of value for money studies (for example, on energy management and catering management); a suite of good practice guides (for example, on risk management, investment decision-making and implementing HR strategies); and data on key resource dimensions (for example, on the estate) (HEFCE 2001a, 2002a, 2002f, 2003a, 2003b, 2003c, 2003d, 2003e).

The most wide-ranging official guide is a rather curious account that purports to offer 'a business approach' to financial strategy (HEFCE 2002d). This document helpfully tries to support the integration of financial thinking with general strategic thinking, and recognizes that doing this well will probably take several years. It also includes some suggested measures of capacity and a set of 'self-challenge questions' that some institutions 'may find daunting', in the way of a '"reality check" on the overall position of the institution and its expenditure in relation both to the income it is generating, and to its position and prospects in the market' (HEFCE 2002d: 10 and 11). There are also references to further sources of information.

External requirements

The planning framework described here makes clear that, as with the data and quality cycles, there are some important external requirements. In some ways, these are different in kind from the requirements applying to data and quality: there is no prescribed format for university strategic or corporate plans and there is no external machinery that seeks to assess, audit or validate them. There is also more debate within the sector about the locus of the funding council in its planning requirements, because of the autonomy of institutions (as well as the centrality of their own strategic plans to the realization of that autonomy) and because of scepticism about the use made of the documentation (PA Consulting 2004b: 20). Paradoxically, therefore, the relationship between those requiring planning information and those providing it can be arguably less smooth than in respect of data and quality. However, the requirements are similarly non-negotiable, particularly when it comes to reporting on activity or progress and on financial matters – notably in the annual monitoring statement, corporate planning statement and financial forecast for HEFCE, and when reporting on the use made of capital and other funds allocated for specific purposes. As we note above, while the planning cycle *should* help to maximize the fit between the HEFCE-required essay to unlock funding and the institution's own view of good practice for its own purposes, this is not always easy.

Reporting on progress

We have emphasized from the start of this book the importance of institutional learning, of evaluating progress as a key component of that learning, and of self-study as a key component of such evaluation. The University of Brighton's planning cycle illustrated in Figure 6.1 involves directly two complementary evaluative outputs – the **Annual Operating Statement** and the **Annual Report** – that in turn inform future plans. It also involves indirectly two other evaluative outputs, and therefore the intersection with the two other institutional cycles, the Annual Academic Health Process (within the quality cycle) and the Annual Academic Year Review (within the data cycle).

The review of progress also has a clear allocation of responsibility for monitoring. Faculty Management Groups monitor progress against the Faculty Plans, Heads of Department lead a review of the plans of their own departments, and each of the thematic strategies is reviewed by a relevant University or Board committee, as set out in Table 6.5.

Table 6.5 University of Brighton: reviewing progress under the thematic strategies

Thematic strategy	Responsible committee of the Board of Governors	Responsible Committee of the Academic Board
Commercial	Finance and Employment	
Estates	Property	Estates
Financial	Finance and Employment	
Information		Information Strategy
Learning and teaching		Learning and Teaching Implementation Group
Research		Research Strategy
Staffing	Finance and Employment	
Widening participation	Board of Governors	Academic Development

This indicates:

- a range of levels and coverage for the various elements of the planning framework;
- clarity of responsibility for reviewing progress;
- external audiences for some of the 'products' of this activity;
- a highly distributed process coordinated by senior consideration of the various elements and progress against them;
- that although the elements of the planning framework can be itemized and considered separately, they relate intimately to each other and cannot be developed or delivered in isolation; and
- linkages to the data and quality cycles.

Here again it is vital that the evaluations reflect the objectives set by the institution itself. There may be a tension here – a recent survey of institutional Heads, for example, noted that the criteria identified by Government for judging the overall health of the sector (participation and progression rates, teaching and research quality, good value for public money) differ from those identified by vice-chancellors as drivers of institutional health (such as staffing, investment funds, cash flow etc.).

(PA Consulting 2004b: 5)

One of the lessons from the Warner and Palfreyman volume in this series is that self-evaluation must also be self-critical, to avoid the kind of 'complacency or even self-delusion' that can lead to a downward spiral into a crisis (Warner and Palfreyman 2003: 7).

The **Annual Operating Statement** is a set of up to thirty targets for the year that the university needs to achieve if it is to achieve its overall Corporate Plan. The targets and progress against them are considered through the planning cycle by the Academic Development Committee, Management Group and Academic Board, before being agreed by the Board of Governors. The targets are grouped under the aims of the Corporate Plan. The final document is disseminated widely internally (and it includes specification of responsibility for work under each item) as well as forming part of the annual monitoring statement submitted to HEFCE.

The **Annual Report**, by contrast, is a more discursive effort. Over recent years, the University's annual report has adopted a format that explicitly addresses progress – and the lack of it – against each of the aims in the Corporate Plan. It is neither at the glossy and obviously 'PR'-oriented end of the spectrum of institutional annual reports nor at the minimalist 'wrap-around' to the accounts, going beyond the minimal but remaining presentationally low-key. It seeks to be relatively self-critical, representing a summation and summary of the various elements of the self-study effort as a whole. It seeks to offer an open account of the university's progress against the aims of its Corporate Plan.

Annual reports over the last few years have included quantitative and qualitative judgements about the university's progress drawn from historical data (over the previous ten years); comparisons with the performance of the comparator universities used by the Board; published performance information; and peer judgements. This enables an assessment of progress, with the implication, often made explicit, that further work is required to achieve the intended outcome.

To be able to report on progress, it is of course first necessary to be able to identify and evaluate progress. We saw in Chapter 4 the interest taken by the Brighton Board of Governors (like others in the

Table 6.6 University of Brighton: evaluating progress

Evaluation item	Against what	Board involvement	Strengths	Weaknesses
A Indicators of performance	Comparator group	Reports to most meetings	Published data; consistent group; some connection possible with Brighton's indicators of success	Dated; not about institutional objectives; limited by what is published; some of the data are vulnerable to collection techniques
B Thematic strategies (e.g. commercial; research; staffing; widening participation)	Objectives in each strategy	Direct for some, via sub-committees; indirect for others, via minutes of committees; also Board seminars on particular themes	Against specific objectives; brought together in Annual Report; high degree of thematic 'ownership'	Have not so far distilled progress for Board; requires discipline on part of receiving committees
C Annual monitoring statement	Targets set in previous year	Considers and signs off targets at June meeting, submitted to HEFCE July	Covers what is important in current year; many of the targets are verifiable; also has commentary on some of the thematic strategies but not all; will previously have been considered by ADC and AB; highly focused	Substantial so not always user-friendly; only looks at one year; may emphasize novel at expense of routine. Board does not see detailed commentaries on progress using HEFCE special funds – but these are looked at in more detail under the thematic headings

Evaluation item	Against what	Board involvement	Strengths	Weaknesses
D Corporate Planning Statement	Corporate Plan aims and objectives	Considers outline at June meeting, submitted to HEFCE July	Summary statement – partly about messages to be conveyed to HEFCE	Purpose may reduce its utility internally; not predominantly for internal use
E Annual Report	Corporate Plan as a whole	Audit Committee and full Board consider draft	Brings together major areas of activity in one statement	Chairman would prefer earlier and formative engagement by the Board in the judgements reached; largely narrative; mixed purposes/audiences (not just for internal self-assessment); will inevitably be high-level
F Corporate Plan indicators of success	Targets in Plan	Through Annual Report, but also brought into PI reports where relevant	Against specific objectives; mostly quantifiable/ verifiable; some use published data so some comparisons would be possible	Needs capacity to remain 'live' if circumstances or policy suggests changes to indicators

Source: Appendix 1 (2004e)

sector) in their ability to do this comparatively, against other universities (Appendix 1 2002c). They have been similarly concerned to be able to play a part in reaching an informed view of progress against the university's own objectives, beyond the immediacy of the annual operating statement. Most recently, the Board has reviewed in a self-critical way how far it 'is able to reach an overall, informed evaluation of the University's progress' (Appendix 1 2004e: i). The Board's view was that there are strengths and weaknesses of the various evaluative elements and that it wanted to augment its work with an additional element that would draw together and relate its considerations directly to the Corporate Plan indicators of success. The resulting approach is shown in Table 6.6, with the new element (F) described. The intention is that the Board will receive the overall analysis in June each year and will be able to concentrate on areas where more work is needed at its first meeting in the subsequent academic year.

We have argued throughout this book that institutional self-study is about more than assisting and informing planning. Nonetheless, the planning cycle will always be the most influential arena for institutional research. Getting it right is a necessary but not a sufficient condition of the reflective community and the learning organization.

PART 3 THE USES OF SELF-STUDY

7

SELF-STUDY AND DECISION-MAKING

This book is about how higher education institutions can use self-study to make better decisions. This chapter identifies both external and internal pressures which can limit or liberate decision-making capacity.

Scanning the horizon

It is a consistent complaint by educational managers that they have relatively little room for manoeuvre. Operating margins in UK HEIs are notoriously tight and there is the increasing phenomenon of micro-management from outside. In these circumstances it is easy for institutional self-study to become too introspective, too reactive, and too defensive against both perceived and real pressures from outside. There is an important, wider part of self-study, which is about how the institution fits into its sector, its host society and the world. Institutions have to maintain a balance between self-study that is 'inside-out' – building on the dynamics of a creative and self-confident community, and 'outside in' – recognizing, adapting to, and where necessary seeking to modify the pressures that bear down upon the modern college or university.

In these circumstances, decision-making begins with the widest possible horizon. Just what is a higher education fit for purpose in the twenty-first century? To return to Walter Lippmann's question in Chapter 3, what are the clusters of 'actual things' upon which we can optimistically build? Four seem particularly important as context for university decision-making.

The first is about the changing ways in which teachers and

researchers view the world, and its resonance with a new generation of students.

A convenient shorthand account of what is going on has been provided by Michael Gibbons and his collaborators. They see an inexorable and irreversible shift from 'mode 1' thinking (pure, disciplinary, homogeneous, expert-led, supply-driven, hierarchical, peer-reviewed, and almost exclusively university-based) to 'mode 2' (applied, problem-centred, transdisciplinary, heterogeneous, hybrid, demand-driven, entrepreneurial, network-embedded etc.) (Gibbons *et al.* 1994).

Several other things fall out of this shift, which affect the university deeply. For example, there is the increasing tendency for leading academics to build alliances: across departments, across institutions, and across national boundaries. There is also the rise of alternative centres of reference – like independent foundations, corporate universities and the 'for-profit' sector – although it is significant how much these newer institutional forms rely on traditional universities to keep them going. And we have been here before: the Open University (now described by UK academics as their proudest achievement in the late twentieth century – conveniently forgetting that at the time they fought it tooth and nail) could not have come into being without sharing intellectual capital (people as well as libraries) with existing universities and colleges.

Students are also at the heart of this transformation. Universities have to respond to the effect of revised preparation and expectations of students, not least as a result of their experience of information and communication technologies (ICT). Jason Frand's seminal essay on the 'information age mind-set' is an arresting account of this dilemma. It is based on the definition by Alan Kay of technology as 'anything that wasn't around when you were born'. All of Frand's 'attributes reflecting values and behaviours' will be familiar to parents of early twenty-first-century screenagers. Our favourite is 'Nintendo not logic'. Others include 'internet better than TV'; 'doing rather than knowing'; 'multi-tasking'; 'typing rather than handwriting'; 'staying connected'; and 'zero tolerance for delays' (Frand 2000).

Sadly the same can't be said of many of their teachers. The Engineering Professors' Conference complains every year about the calculus that first-year students could do twenty years ago but can't now. They never look at the reciprocal. Just what skills do this new generation bring with them that their predecessors didn't, and how relevant are they? Another facet of this changing culture is student paid work: the modern undergraduate (like the modern sixth-former) regularly works for money, and not just to eat. It's also a significant lifestyle choice, further distancing us from that evocative definition of higher education (by Michael Oakeshott) as 'the gift of an interval'.

There are other concerns about the motivation of participants. Does the market rule – in students' minds, or in the minds of those funding the expansion? Student demand does indeed reflect a swing towards greater vocational and career sensitivity than in the past. This is, of course, rational behaviour. In the elite, restricted systems of the past, graduates achieved market salience simply by having a degree. These days what that degree is in – and its utility – is much more important. In the UK we have recently had some serious swings in student choice of subjects. The winners include health, computing and media studies; while the losers have been the natural sciences, technology and building. And institutions have found it hard to adjust, or have perhaps been reluctant to try.

To return to student rationality, we probably underestimate the extent to which young people have more realistic (as well as more ambitious) views about where their careers and lives may go than those which are held for them by many colleges and universities (as well as by other interested parties like employers and politicians). Above all, they have come to mistrust narrow or apparently end-stopped vocational qualifications. For many, for example those choosing IT or media-related courses, there seems to be a lot in Richard Florida's thesis about *The Rise of the Creative Class* (2000).

Florida finds in the recent history of the United States both a new (Marxist-style) mode of production and a new (related) 'creative class'. These are people 'in science and engineering, architecture and design, education, arts, music and entertainment, whose economic function is to create new ideas, new technology and/or creative content'. According to his analysis they now comprise 30 per cent of all employed people (with a 'super-creative' core of 12 per cent), leaving only 20 per cent in the traditional working class, and a clear new majority in the fast-rising 'service class' of occupations like personal care, food service and new-style clerical functions such as call centres.

Students and staff have thus collaborated to create a new kind of university community, and this provides a second 'cluster.'

How does this link with the student instrumentality mentioned above? In a fascinating study, John Ahier and his collaborators have tested the views of their 'future lives as employees and citizens' held by final-year students at two neighbouring but very different universities (Cambridge and Anglia Polytechnic). Most importantly, a strong focus on employment and careers does not appear to have corroded this generation of students' powerful sense of a 'social sphere' in which they are morally responsible actors. Analysing the students' relationship to peers, to other generations, to 'abstract others' such as welfare recipients, and to formal and constitutional authorities, the authors found that 'these circuits were governed by principles such as fairness, altruism, reciprocity and responsibility', which they sum up 'in the more general term "mutuality"' (Ahier *et al.* 2002: 141). In other words, while the current generation of British students – like many elsewhere in the world – have to think long and hard about their economic life chances, it is crude and inaccurate to typecast them as 'Thatcher's children' or the 'Organization Kid'.

This may be an unfairly maligned generation of students. For the Confederation of British Industry (CBI) and Institute of Directors (IoD), too many of them have chosen to become graduates rather than plumbers; as if they can't be both. For political leaders, they have turned their backs on party politics; but they care deeply, about each other and, for example, about international justice and environmental responsibility. For social activists, they have apparently fixated on jobs and postgraduate prospects rather than traditional 'volunteering'; but they are among the first generations of British graduates who know that the world does not owe them a living.

Substantial longitudinal studies carry the same message. The Wider Benefits of Learning Group at the Institute of Education has been tracking the experience of the 1958 National Childhood Development Study and the 1970 British Cohort Study. Their findings are dramatic. Despite the considerable expansion of the UK graduate population, and after carefully controlling for other possible influences, graduates retain significant benefits in the 'domains of health, the labour market, citizenship and parenthood'. This is not all rocket science: graduates are, for example, much more likely to read to their children. Meanwhile, it is also important to acknowledge a worm in the apple. Students from poorer backgrounds who start a full-time HE course and then drop out fall behind their non-participating peers in almost all of these respects (HEFCE 2001e; Bynner *et al.* 2003; Schuller *et al.* 2004).

Next, it is important to consider the teacher's perspective. Cultural and other changes in the student body have been matched by shifts in the demography and organization of the academic profession itself. A survey by the UK funding councils shows that, as the profession grows, it has become younger (the average age in the UK is now 41), and its members are more likely to have had experience outside as well as inside the academy (HEFCE 2002e). The main message is about the combined effects of generational change and of expansion. As a 'lump' of academics brought into the profession by an earlier phase of expansion retires simultaneously with the

recruitment of the next expansion-fuelled 'lump' (in student numbers and the range of university activity), turnover will be rapid. In
these circumstances, 'internal' socialization is likely to weaken and
new perspectives to gain greater purchase. It is important to stress
(again) that this is happening all over the world. The country with
probably the biggest challenge of renewal is Canada, where the
average age today is 49 (AUCC 2002: 28–31).

One effect – already felt around the system – is the breakdown of
traditional assumptions about the separation of 'academic' and
'support' roles. Learners are now critically dependent upon modern
librarians, computing officers and technicians, as well as knowl-
edgeable welfare and advice services. Institutions have had to move
past benign amateurism to pull themselves together in terms of
finance, estates, personnel and marketing and public relations.

In the spirit of institutional self-study, bringing these forces together is, of course, part of the critical role of university leaders. How
well are they doing?

When they gather in victim support groups like Universities UK,
heads of institutions will readily agree about the pressures bearing
down on them. Here, for example, is the list of key predictions made
by university leaders at a consultation event organized by the European University Association and the American Council on Education in late 2002. This is what US, Canadian and European university
heads said was going to happen to us:

- greater emphasis on the HE role in workforce preparation than in
  social development and cultural identity;
- more 'borderless' provision;
- policy interest in HE as a social investment;
- more partnerships with business and 'non-educational'
  organizations;
- government insistence on accountability through 'outcome-
  orientated quality assessments';
- access dependent upon technology because 'traditional modes of
  instruction cannot fill the need';
- increased competition and market forces but scepticism about
  'brand-name' domination;
- national governments to maintain their influence;
- increase in instruction in English;
- governance and decision-making patterns inhibiting the 'institutions' ability to change'; and
- significant increase in inter-institutional collaboration.

(EUA/ACE 2002)

If these first two clusters of 'actual things' are an accurate reflection of reality, we may be in danger of overestimating the extrinsic influences and underestimating the intrinsic influences on the development of the university in the knowledge society.

If correct, this thesis has some important consequences for what vice-chancellors, presidents, and the like are trying to do. For example, dealing successfully with external influences – as it were 'from above' – in the interests of preserving the status quo (i.e. achieving 'institutional comfort') may turn out to be a hollow victory, if the internal pressures for change – as it were 'from below' – have meanwhile transformed the system. There is a familiar danger here: of generals fighting the last war, of industrialists solving yesterday's problems, and of politicians listening only to each other.

A third set of understandings through which students are in many instances ahead of their teachers is about the global inter-connectedness of what they could and should be doing.

First there is the issue of global competitiveness. All around the world the rhetoric – and most of the action – seems to be about global higher education as a simple market, and the resulting bottom line for institutions and their investors. Selling places in higher education is now in the top ten export earners for all of the G8 countries (Fielden 2003). But at what cost? There are some profound ethical questions here.

There is, for example, the damage done by colonial-style intervention which 'substitutes' for traditional university functions in developing countries. An example is in research, where as David King, the Chief Scientific Adviser, has recently pointed out, a sound domestic capacity is needed to pull through a properly qualified academic work force, including the supply of teachers further down the educational hierarchy (King 2002). We are in danger – especially in the UK – of turning our back on a proud record of assisting less developed university systems to progress. Meanwhile, the record of European and North American models of intellectual property rights can often be seen by these systems as a pre-emptive strike, if not asset-stripping. Even more immediately, there is the danger of saturation of domestic markets by under-priced and sometimes shoddy goods in the form of e-learning; one of the strongest findings of market research by the short-lived UK e-university is of resentment of the poor quality of so much of the material that is being made available in this way. Finally, and in the long term perhaps most serious, is the lack of formal attention to those parts of the modern university curriculum that should support global citizenship. Many British universities now have students from over one hundred countries outside the UK. Are we listening to them?

Political forces are, of course, at work here. As universities are enlisted into the armies of national competitiveness and social cohesion, who are the real generals? The temptation is for the politicians to steer from outside, and for university leaders to collude when they think it suits them. The danger then is that we tell neither truth to power, nor truth to ourselves.

There is a related pathology, which also has international resonance: the almost universal political sense that the grass has to be greener somewhere else; that there is some essential element of another national system which is more attractive and effective than your own. The problem is that national higher education systems come in packages. They are, as John Kay says of markets, 'culturally embedded' (Kay, 2003).

To take an example: the current UK government is obsessed with the US. They would like market-driven variability, but they would not want many of the other things that would come with it. Most importantly, they would have to be more tolerant of delayed completion. F. Scott Fitzgerald said that there are no second acts in American lives; there are certainly second colleges. Fifty-nine per cent of graduates with first degrees have earned them with credit from more than one institution. They would also have to acknowledge an abandonment of professional formation at the 'first-cycle' or undergraduate level. And they would have to accept weakening of quality control, of other aspects of consumer protection, and of the controlled reputational range which is one of the UK system's proudest achievements.

Fourthly, as a number of authoritative commentators have recently reminded us, the pendulum has swung in this discussion too far from the public interest in higher education, and too far towards the private interest. In a recent lecture to the Higher Education Policy Institute, Robert Reich set out the stark history of decline in the United States of what he called the 'mission of public education': of 'public investment for a public return'; of mobilization of the most talented members of society for the good of society; and 'of social leadership in a more complex world' (Reich 2004).

The hot technical question here is about personal vs. social rates of return, and all of the confusion that surrounds the economic analysis of externalities. Higher educational achievement – like all educational achievement – is a positional good. Consequently, at what point does public investment (or shared risk) reach its optimum level, and personal obligation (or individual risk) kick in?

The UK is not the only nation where this issue has become hugely politically contentious. The evidence points in different directions. There are the 'wider benefits' of learning to which we have alluded. There is also the evidence of unsatisfied demand for higher level skills. There is the growing penetration by graduates of occupations where there have never been graduates before (one commentator's 'under-employment' is another's 'growing the job'). And then there are the hugely varied and speculative extrapolations of a 'graduate' premium of enhanced lifetime earnings.

But is there another social cost here? The more people have this 'positional good', the less distinctive the asset is. But at the same time the gulf between those with and those without the asset increases. Increasing social polarization may be one of those areas where higher education is simultaneously part of the problem and part of the solution.

In strategic terms, for institutions and for the higher education sector, this is where 'skills' meets 'widening participation'. Assessing the evidence base is tricky.

Under careful analysis most of this problem reverts to polarization, between the (commendably growing) proportion of society which stays engaged and succeeds, and the increasingly isolated but stubbornly significant minority who fall off, and don't get back on:

- the 50 per cent of the population who don't achieve Level 2 (GCSE-equivalent) qualifications;
- the 20 per cent who leave Level 3 (A2-equivalent) with low achievements; and
- the 9 per cent who drop out of education, employment and training altogether somewhere between 14 and 19. According to the Paul Hamlyn National Commission on Education Follow-up Group, 'the figure rises to . . . 24 per cent of the total if those in jobs but receiving no education or training are added' (NCE 2003: 11).

The same powerful influence of class continues at Level 2. In the UK we know that 90 per cent of students with two or more A levels go on to higher education. We also know that only 45 per cent of those with vocational qualifications at this level proceed. The big trap in the UK at the moment is the illusion that 'aiming higher' and 'widening participation' are the same thing. Table 7.1 presents another take on this A level data. Note that the bottom group has fewer successes, and lower achievement, but the same progression rate with that achievement.

Solving this 'big' problem and the 'smaller' problems which make it up is going to require attention to both 'push' factors (chiefly about motivation) and 'pull' factors (chiefly about provision and systems).

Table 7.1 UK education experience by socio-economic group, 2002

	Less affluent background (III manual, IV and V)	More affluent background (I, II, and III non-manual)
Percentage gaining 2+ A/AS levels	23%	47%
subdivided into		
25+ points	6% (26%)	18% (38%)
13–24 points	11% (48%)	21% (45%)
1–12 points	6% (26%)	8% (17%)
Percentage entering HE		
25+ points	71%	73%
13–24 points	57%	62%
1–12 points	45%	45%

Note: percentage of 18-year-olds in each group

Source: Youth Cohort Study www.data-archive.ac.uk/findingData/yesTitles.asp (Cohort 10, sweep 3, 18-year-olds in 2002)

Among the things we need to consider at the national level are the levers of positive change, including:

• funding – of learners as well as providers;
• qualification frameworks – a common credit currency; 14–19 reform; academic, vocational and mixed forms;
• employment – especially employers' 'buy-in' to training.

But we also have to ask some cultural questions. Educational systems are, as suggested above, 'culturally embedded' – what are the implications of wanting to look like, for example:

• Singapore – a society constructed around success in very traditional public examinations;
• or the United States – with its huge Community College network;
• or Australia – with its centrally driven technical and further education (TAFE) system;
• or Germany – where, contrary to many people's belief, students now regularly use intermediate level vocational qualifications to re-enter 'academic' or general higher education?

Table 7.2 represents a reality check, about the qualifications and commitment of managers in some of these societies.

Table 7.2 Education and training of management

Item	UK	US	Japan	Germany	France
Average terminal education age (1999, years)	19.5	22	21	21	22
Graduate (%)	49	74	78	72	61
Days off-the-job training (1998)	4	7	5.5	5.5	6
Days on-the-job training (1998)	4.5	8	6.5	6.5	6

Source: Keep and Westwood in CIHE (2004:10)

This leads on to further hard questions about those interests of civil society which may be opposed to the state (or the ruling power) itself. Michael Daxner, former Rector of the University of Oldenburg and European Union Commissioner for Higher Education in post-war Kosovo, has put the point eloquently. 'East of Vienna', he says, 'the role of universities has to be in society-making, not state-making' (Daxner 2002). In some of the more comfortable parts of the world we have to be conscious of the experience elsewhere of universities being sucked into state priorities which might violate all that they stand for.

The fundamental problem is perhaps that too many people currently think that they 'own' too much of the university. The state won't achieve its objectives unless it is prepared to live with genuine institutional autonomy. The other stakeholders need to understand that if they are to live up to this designation, they have to put something at risk. The traditional view is that the university belongs fundamentally to its members: the *collegium* (and, since 1992, the corporation). However, above all, if we are right, the collegium cannot stand still. If it is to survive and prosper, it will have to continue the historical process of reinventing itself.

The encouraging thing is that the HE system has done this before, and can do it again.

Drawing these wider, horizon-scanning issues back into the university or college itself, the current debate centres on the problem of choosing a mission from an acceptable and viable range of options. The HEFCE *Strategic Plan* apparently sets out a range of options, based upon its 'core + margin' approach, redescribed as 'supporting institutions to focus on achieving excellence in what they do best and to collaborate based on their strengths' (HEFCE 2004b: 30). However, several strong institutions (notably those from among the 'non-aligned' group identified by the UUK Longer Term Strategy Group) find this hard to live with. We noted earlier that one of the policy lessons from the UUK's data is that, to meet national objectives, it seems essential that government continues to support institutions across the reputational range.

The decision tree ▮

Strategic decision-making in universities and colleges is rarely dramatic, and those who lead it are rarely cast as heroic. There are one or two exceptions to this which prove the rule, like the decision by the then City of Birmingham Polytechnic (now the University of Central England) not to participate in the 1992 Research Assessment Exercise (RAE), or the merger of the Guildhall and North London Universities to produce London Metropolitan University in 2002.

Most institutional decisions would be regarded elsewhere in the corporate world as 'nudges' rather than clear changes of direction, and there are good reasons for this including the length of the product cycle, the prescriptive conditions attached to funding, and the heavy investment in specialist staff and infrastructure. Such nudges are usually about academic shape (the subject and 'level' base of the course portfolio) and about the balance of activity (typically between 'teaching', 'research' and the 'third leg' [or 'arm'] of service to business and the community, covered by the more felicitous American term 'service').

The main device for such nudges is that of *creative, temporary cross-subsidy*. All of the significant terms in this non-heroic summary of strategic leadership are necessary; none is sufficient by itself.

Good scoping, as well as a sense of history, should enable the well-informed institution to achieve the necessary balance between continuity and change. In turn this should lead to the articulation of a **mission statement** which is both ambitious and realistic.

The mission will then drive the principal **activity areas** of a university or college, namely:

- the academic portfolio (subjects, courses and modes of study);
- research and professional development; and
- the 'third leg' (or arm) of business and community service.

Underpinning these activities will be a whole series of **enabling decision fields**. Examples are:

- human resources (including staff development);
- choice of collaborators or partners;
- financial and investment strategies;
- academic infrastructure (including libraries and networks); and
- development of the estate.

All levels of this tree can be informed by evidence: prospectively (as in scoping); concurrently (as in monitoring); and retrospectively (as in institutional research). The trick is to align optimally the three cycles described in Part 2.

Meanwhile, the goals of institutional self-study include not only better strategic choices but also winning hearts and minds, inside and outside the institution; in other words, the art of persuasion. The trick is to get the evidence, and to use the evidence to support the decision before the persuasion begins. The 'report on progress' items in Part 2 are intended to be contributions to this process. They also underline how far 'institutional character' (as discussed in Chapter 9) is bound up in the question of effective communication – not only in the committee room, but also in the corridor.

Achieving good performance in this respect is easier to say than to do. There is a real trap inherent in reaching a conclusion and then searching for evidence to support it; a trap compounded by the frequent failure of evidence about educational achievement to reach a firm conclusion. A good example is graduate employability, where the advocates of both more graduates and fewer graduates to serve the national interest can go to the literature and find studies to support their competing points of view (CIHE/AIM 2004).

One of the most difficult issues is that of getting the unit of analysis right, for different purposes. The analysis so far in this book has ranged, Russian doll-style, from the course or project, through the department or School, and then to the institution, the region, the nation and the world. All of these levels are interconnected, but lessons from one may not be immediately applicable to another. Above all, as will be discussed in the next chapter, there is the question of how far self-knowledge at each of these levels can improve self-confidence (internally) and reputational enhancement (externally).

In a field of activity as complex and contingent as the management of a university or college, good decision-making will always rely at least as much on judgement as on empirical analysis. 'Wicked issues' abound, and there are certainly no formulae to follow. Similarly, a less than perfect decision can often spring a satisfactory result if it has the whole-hearted support of the community which has to live with it. Serious and systematic self-study can, however, narrow the field of risk and, even more importantly, create the circumstances in which success or failure can be objectively understood, to then be built upon or adjusted.

8

SELF-STUDY AND REPUTATION

This book is about how institutions can use self-study to choose and then support their position within the sector and within their various 'markets'. This chapter unpacks the delicate issue of institutional reputation.

The reputational reservoir

Managing institutional reputation is probably the most important duty of university and college leaders. Institutional reputation itself rests upon a delicate balance of components, one of the most important of which is history. The *reputational reservoir* is critical to the maintenance of institutional health, as is the direction of travel on what might be called the **risk cycle**.

Briefly, the risk cycle starts characteristically with bad news, say a financial disaster, a whistle-blower's scandal, or simply the bad luck to be where an epidemic breaks out or a gruesome murder occurs (these are all true stories in British universities). This leads to one or more of the various 'business failures' to which a university or college is vulnerable: a drop in recruitment; a decline in research contracts; or the withdrawal of key clients and partners. The fall in income, coupled with a reduced rating for borrowing or a downturn in discretionary earnings such as endowments, leads to a degradation of the infrastructure as it is perceived by students, staff and other stakeholders. This in turn leads to more bad news; and so on. The direction of travel is downwards, and can be very hard to decelerate, arrest or reverse.

The element that can slow down a downward spiral is the reservoir of positive reputation held at the time of the bad news. This has certainly helped the University of Cambridge to maintain its leading position in public esteem despite a collection of episodes which, for others, would probably prove disastrous: budget deficits; a huge overrun on a failing new financial system (CAPSA); negative reports from the National Audit Office (NAO) on a high-profile, politically inspired initiative (the Cambridge–MIT project); rejection by the Senate of key elements of governance reform; expensive litigation with a staff member over an eventually achieved promotion; and prosecution by the Health & Safety Executive. Incidentally, none of these appears (except the first, without comment) in the university's glossy *Annual Report 2003*. Shattock, in his external report on the CAPSA affair, commented wryly that Harvard and Stanford would be 'unlikely to tolerate the implicit suggestion [of several of his witnesses] that their governance and management should be permitted to be less effective because their universities are outstandingly successful academically' (Shattock 2001: 1.3). It is worth reflecting on the potential impact of even one of these 'bad news' items on any other university.

Nonetheless, building the reputational reservoir is a vital part of institutional strategy, as those institutions with a weaker record facing hard times (say, Luton or Thames Valley) would attest. Above all there is the possibility of instigating and then maintaining a virtuous (or upward) spiral – from good news, to stronger performance, to improved infrastructure, and so on – through the exact reverse of the process described above. Having an honest sense of which direction you are going in is a potentially valuable product of self-study.

Most of this is about one of the newest arrivals in the pantheon of corporate responsibilities (although, like many of the others, it is a new set of terms for a deeply historical set of functions), namely **risk management**. The chief virtue of institutional self-study in the field of risk is that it helps you to write it down.

That said, it is often the 'out of left field' issues that constitute the highest potential impact risks for a university or college. From detailed attention to the operation of and messages from the cycles of performance data, of quality assurance, and of strategic and operational planning should spring both well-informed analysis of risk, and often of its remedy. At the University of Brighton such 'routine' risks and remediation moved significantly down the list when the local council decided that a site, immediately contiguous to our sole green-field campus, was the optimum location for the local Football League Club's new stadium.

It is, of course, a human inclination to want, in the words of Johnny Mercer and Harold Arlen (for the *Jungle Book*), to 'Accentuate the positive/Eliminate the negative/Latch on to the affirmative/ Don't mess with Mister In-between'. But there are two traps here: one internal, the other external. Self-delusion is a trap, as is the ethical danger of misleading the public.

On the latter, the Institute of Business Ethics has issued Ten Commandments, in the context of identifying best practice in managing reputation risk. A shortened version follows:

- clear vision ('what we stand for');
- clear values supported by a code of ethics or conduct;
- policies clearly stating performance expectations and risk tolerance in key areas;
- detailed understanding of major stakeholders' expectations, information requirements and perceptions of the organization;
- an open, trusting, supportive culture;
- a robust and dynamic risk management system;
- organizational learning ... leading to corrective action;
- reward and recognition systems which support the organization's goals and values;
- extension of vision and values to joint venture and outsource partners and major suppliers;
- meaningful, open and honest dialogue and communications tailored to meet the needs of specific stakeholder groups.

(IBE 2001: 41)

An attempt to tailor such expectations to the circumstances of HEIs has been made by the Council for Industry and Higher Education (CIHE 2004).

As usual with exercises of this kind, there is an element of counselling perfection. However, it does provide a salutary reality check for the particular circumstances of an HEI. How ready, for example, is the average university to check on the performance in these respects of academic, let alone commercial or industrial partners?

Asking the right questions

The most important injunction is probably to define, and then not to duck, the hard questions. Here are five, regarded as particularly sensitive at the University of Brighton. As will be quickly apparent, they are all multi-dimensional, they are all susceptible to both qualitative and quantitative analysis, and they all require mature judgement about defining and making choices for future development.

- Have we got our academic portfolio right, in terms of subjects, levels, learning and teaching approaches, and so on?
- What is the right research strategy for a university like ours, focused mainly on 'professional formation'?
- What should our approach be to collaboration, to partnerships, and ensuring the health, not just of the University of Brighton, but of the wider education service and of our communities?
- Assuming we know more and more about *what* we have achieved, do we also know what more we *could have* achieved? (Do we, for example, fully understand value for money, opportunity costs, and performance potential?)
- In terms of 'who we are', what should our ambitions be for 'reputational positioning'; how do these relate to the emergence across UK higher education of sub-sectoral special interest groups (including the Russell Group, the 94 Group, and the Coalition of Mainstream Universities) or indeed the emerging regional agenda?

Information for students

Whatever measures emerge to support conclusions in response to these and similar questions are also being used by others to generate comparative conclusions, notably in newspaper **league tables**, commercial **guides for students**, and now by the government following a commitment in the 2003 White Paper to a **national student survey** (NSS). Data supplied by a variety of bodies are all grist to these particular mills:

- by HESA in the form of annual reports as well as in response to specific research requests;
- by UCAS in their sphere of activity;
- by the judgements of the QAA (although these are largely qualitative, crude attempts can be made to develop 'scores' – for example of the number of points for 'attention' or 'commendation');
- 'by the institutions in standard form following the Cooke Report'; and
- by the Funding Council in publishing performance indicators on an annual basis as well as periodic data such as the results of the RAE.

The iniquities and the inevitability of league tables are now well documented (Bowden 2000). The most frustrating element is probably the statistical illiteracy of combining scores derived from differing (and frequently mutually contradictory bases) into a single rank. Then there is the disguised (and normally conservative) choice of the key determining elements and their spuriously scientific weighting. But they are an increasing part of the higher education market – in services as well as for students – and there is evidence that, perversely, their use increases the more sophisticated the audience: the 2003 UNITE survey showed only 21 per cent claiming to have used league tables to help them choose a university, but this covers 25 per cent of social classes AB and only 16 per cent of C2DE (UNITE 2003: 15). So institutions need to get their retaliation in first; and self-study can help.

All of the national broadsheet newspapers now publish their own league tables, using the same volume-related data purchased from HESA (and therefore the source is the data provided by institutions themselves). But they have subtle – and sometimes less subtle – differences in the way they treat the data, and the outcomes tend to reflect the assumed predilections of their readers. Thus the *Guardian* version includes data on widening participation, a calculation of value added and does not include research scores, whereas the *Times* weightings prioritize research. In addition, the *Guardian* offers rankings at subject level; the *Telegraph* offers a combined 'table of tables'.

There is now a guide on how to use these publications, from UCAS, aimed at students and their parents/advisers. The Foreword is instructive:

> there is an irresistible urge to classify and categorise knowledge. We analyse, measure and sort the information which is available to us, partly to make it more manageable and, sometimes, in order to make statements about the relative worth of something which is important to us.
>
> (Greatrix 2003: 1)

Reasons given for the production of the guide include the following:

- league tables reflect the twin drives for accountability and consumer information;
- they attempt rankings but the way they adapt data into numerical scores and the way they construct their weightings are opaque and could never reflect the individual interest of intending students, and can be misleading if used uncritically;
- users therefore need an impartial guide.

Reading the guide reveals a strenuous (but perhaps currently hopeless) attempt systematically to debunk the assumption that the universities at the top of the published tables are necessarily 'the best' and to question the relationship between ranking and actual student experience. In effect, the guide is a valuable critique of the data collections themselves and what they tell us, as well as how they are used by the compilers of the tables. It notes, for example, the volatility of some data between years; the fallacy of converting verbal descriptors of quality into numerical scores; differences between institutions in how effectively they collect some data and in how they report it; and that much of the difference in league table position is explicable by differences in inputs and in context, whether of students or of subject mix. (There is a useful table comparing the main criteria used in the league tables on page 16 and a glossary of terms on pages 26 and 27 of the 2003 *Guide*.) It notes, above all, that these league tables should be treated with caution because 'most of the criteria used do not offer any guide to the actual quality of education provided', but that consistency between the various tables 'is seen by many to be a reasonable indication of a university's or college's *overall standing* in UK higher education' (Greatrix 2003: 17 and 19, emphasis added). So what we have, then, is a set of information purporting to support student choice that is in fact more about status than the student experience.

Indeed, research in both the US and UK shows that most of the variation in the outcomes represented in the league tables is accounted for by variation in the inputs. A critique of the influential *US News and World Report* league tables notes, for example, that the scores are 'insensitive to different student populations among institutions' (Gater 2002: 6). The most convincing explanation for what is going on here is also the simplest. Multi-factoral league tables, like that published by *The Times*, are in fact purely circular. Creation of the so-called 'prosperity' table, based on dividing the income from all sources of an HEI by its full-time equivalent students, predicts the *Times* table with stunning accuracy (a regular correlation between the two in excess of 0.9): prosperity rules (Watson and Bowden 1999 and 2002: 31).

We noted earlier the argument that providing information for students that informs their choices will work to drive up standards in the sector. The Scottish funding councils' joint corporate plan 2003–06 notes 'student choice will remain the single largest factor driving the direction of the system; it is essential that it be as well informed as possible' (SFCFHE 2003: 6). The 2003 White Paper argued that student choice will be an increasingly important driver of teaching quality, as students choose the good-quality courses that will bring them respected and valuable qualifications and give them the higher-level skills that they will need during their working life. But student choice can only drive up quality successfully if it is underpinned by robust information – otherwise reputations will be built on perception rather than reality ... to become intelligent customers of an increasingly diverse provision, and to meet their own increasing diverse needs, students need accessible information. We will ensure that the views of students themselves are published in a national annual survey ... we will also expect institutions to make progress on their own internal systems for securing student feedback.

(DfES 2003: 4.1–4.2)

Much of this is reflected in the Cooke report and the decision to use the HERO web portal as the repository of qualitative and quantitative information about institutions. The intention is to draw as much data as possible automatically from existing sources, providing templates and common definitions for the presentation of data, and linking readily to institutional websites. The data to be available via HERO include for each institution, at the level of nineteen subject areas:

- entry qualifications;
- continuation data;
- qualification data; and
- employment data.

There is also to be a set of qualitative information including a summary of the learning and teaching strategy, summaries of external examiner reports and accounts of links with employers (HEFCE 2003e). This is, of course, as we have noted previously, part of a wider government drive to use consumer choice – based on better performance data – to help in the modernization agenda. However, some of this is questionable in terms of the effort involved and the efficacy of the results. The Nuffield Trust, for example, has published a fascinating and challenging account of the difficulties of involving NHS patients in making qualitative judgements about their care, which is salutary in respect of the impact of power relations and the capacity of 'service users' to interrogate performance data in a meaningful way (Nuffield Trust 2003). Work in higher education is ongoing but forceful: as we noted in Chapter 5, one of the aspects reviewed in the new QAA institutional audit framework addresses the 'accuracy, integrity, completeness and frankness of the information that an institution publishes about the quality of its programmes and the standards of its awards' as they move towards the new information regime (QAA 2002b: 3). The report on the first round of these audits notes that the majority of the eight HEIs included are making good progress towards meeting the new expectations, but that one faces a significant challenge in so doing (QAA 2003a).

Institutions' responses to the initial Cooke proposals questioned the resource effort and, by implication, the value for money that would be achieved (while student groups were generally more positive) (HEFCE 2002b). The pilot report noted that the likely set-up cost to the sector of the suite of proposals would be £4–7m, largely in staff time and in changes to institutional systems, with recurrent annual costs at about £5–8m (including payments to external examiners for additional work) (HEFCE 2003f: 16). The pilot also noted doubts about the accessibility of the data to some of its intended users, as well as about the validity of the conclusions that might be drawn (HEFCE 2003e). The national survey of final year students (NSS), now due for 2005, needs to address the variable institutional response rate of the pilot (which ranged from 26 to 70.5 per cent). Even the hearty 40 per cent average response rate may be insufficient to generate confidence in the results, particularly for smaller subject groups at individual institutions (Richardson 2004). Overall, however, there is room for optimism here – the pilot appears to indicate a workable model for the NSS and relatively low cost to institutions (depending on the volume of follow-up necessary), with results that have the potential to indicate both perceived differences between subjects and institutions and reassuringly high levels of overall student satisfaction.

'Positioning' and 'marketing'

Inside the institution, the people most interested in apparently empirically validated good news are, of course, the marketing department. Most undergraduate prospectuses now include a section on 'why Poppleton' (or wherever)? This is usually couched around so-called 'unique selling points', which have a disturbing propensity to be not unique at all. Here is the set in the University of Brighton 2005 undergraduate prospectus, under the heading 'What we can offer you':

- Excellent teaching – the basis of our reputation and your career;
- Research of international quality – underpinning or contributing to your course;
- Flexibility and diversity – relevant to your circumstances and goals;
- Professional recognition and exemptions from professional examinations;
- Graduate employment – one of the best places to launch your career;
- The study-environment – cutting-edge facilities to maximise your progress;
- The location – welcome to the unique city-by-the-sea.

(Appendix 1 2004b)

Judicious text follows each of these temptations, but few numbers (although most can be crudely validated by statistical analysis). It is, of course, a responsibility of management not to let the 'spin' get out of control (as it has done from time to time). Nonetheless a forensic scholar could have an awful lot of fun with this and similar statements. First of all, they are a mixture of the descriptive and the evaluative. Secondly, they are generated as much by external expectations (what the punters want) as internal imperatives (what we have to offer). Thirdly, they are selective in their use of benchmarking. Fourthly, they juxtapose characteristics in the control of the university (like the curriculum) with those much more serendipitous (like cultural environment – and there is another university in the 'city-by-the-sea').

But it has to be said that it works. As the *Education Guardian* says in its 'What's it like to work at . . .?' series, 'Brighton rocks' (*Education Guardian* 2003).

Not that there is any shortage of expensive advice in this area. The firm Communications Management recently commissioned Chris Chapleo of Roehampton Institute to find out that 'almost all chief executives feel reputation/brand management is a critical issue', and that 'university leaders feel there are huge barriers they must overcome before they can successfully build brands'. It's no surprise to learn that position in 'rankings' is seen as one of the platforms or barriers for success, nor the following list of items perceived to have the most likely impact on reputation:

- differential tuition fees;
- research funding mechanisms;
- government agenda for differential 'missions';
- customer service approaches; and
- mergers and alliances.

(Chapleo 2003: 5, 11, 12)

A similar exercise by the recruitment advertising agency Barkers has a rather stronger empirical base. In 2001 they undertook a survey published as *The Binary Line Revisited*, which concluded (despite the efforts of UCAS and others alluded to above) that the distinction between pre- and post-92 universities remained highly salient for applicant students and their families, nearly a decade on (Barkers 2001). Subsequently, in 2003, they have probed further the 'relevance of reputation'. The most interesting conclusion is how far apart can be perception of reputation and action (as in choice). They conclude (on the basis of surveying nearly 5000 students in eleven institutions) as follows.

- Teaching quality is 'the most important component of reputation', followed closely by the perception of how much money the institution invests in its academic infrastructure (libraries, computers and staff). Promisingly, one-third claimed now to be indifferent to the 'old' and 'new' university designation, although three-quarters identified teaching quality with high entry qualifications.
- League tables are beginning to have an interestingly ambivalent effect. 82 per cent saw them as an influential component of reputation but 77 per cent said that they were not important in making a choice of university (social scientists might identify an element of self-regard in this anomaly).
- The interaction between the attraction of the course, the location and the environment is key to undergraduate choices. This combination easily beats 'reputation', cited by only 535 as influencing their final choice. (It is interesting to note that the UNITE 2004 survey reaches the same conclusion: the 'course offered' is a first mention – 68 per cent – followed only then by 'academic reputation' – 44 per cent [UNITE 2004: 7].)
- Institutions will have to work harder for repeat business. Only 25 per cent continue in the same institution from undergraduate to postgraduate study.
- Postgraduate choices depend much more on an individual assessment of academic facilities, and especially contact and support. These can trump both RAE scores and research income.
- Fewer than one-third of students (29.9 per cent) consider that their universities possess a 'brand'.
- As has been confirmed by a succession of reports (UNITE etc.), most respondents are highly satisfied, and over 80 per cent would recommend their university to others.

(Barkers 2003)

The reactions to evidence like this can vary. There will be an element of 'more research needed' (see Chapter 2) and of surprise at the counter-intuitive (see Chapter 9). There may also be casual disregard of some of the lessons, for example about securing repeat business, which in principle has to be a good thing. Probably the most important injunction is to continue to address these and related questions from the perspective of your own institution. The University of Brighton has begun to put together evidence from both its annual survey of why students choose the university (now eight years old) and a more recently instituted 'decliners' survey'. The overall response in 2003–04 matches the Barkers' survey in volume (c. 5000). Positive conclusions include the huge influence of the perception of the content and style of the course, and how far it matches what the student is looking for, particularly if reinforced by experience of an open day (Appendix 1 2003d, 2003e, 2004d). 'Decliners not only cite the opposite conclusion, but are also refreshingly honest when they have used the University as an "insurance" choice' (Appendix 1 2004d).

All of this points to the knowledge created by self-study not only contributing to making institutions more free (in terms of choosing from competing options on an informed basis), but also more honest (in terms of telling the truth not only to their clients but also to themselves).

9

AN INSTITUTIONAL BALANCE
SHEET

*This book is about how an institution goes about creating an authentic
account of itself. Previous chapters have described some of the techniques and
frameworks used by one university (the authors' own) to do this in a
systematic way. This chapter offers an overall assessment of how the
university strives to know itself, its problems and its possibilities, illustrating
this with a case study about student retention.*

Capacity and coverage

One way of getting at an institutional balance sheet, as we noted in
Chapter 2, is to assess practice on two dimensions: institutional
capacity for self-study and self-study coverage, where the further
behind the 'actual' score is from the 'desired' score, the worse the
performance on each dimension. On this basis, the Brighton
experience suggests the following:

- *on capacity*, the University has relatively strong technical knowledge but needs to improve its internal benchmarking; while
- in relation to *coverage*, there is a good range of intelligence, with
  that on research and teaching performance pretty much meeting
  current needs, but gaps remain in understanding costs and the
  market. In particular, the Board of Governors continues to require
  a coherent overview of aspects of comparative performance, both
  against University objectives and against other universities.

As we have suggested throughout this book, this all indicates a
degree of common ground between the experiences and perception

of the University of Brighton and the sector more generally, as evidenced from surveys of management information systems from QAA institutional audit reports, from discussions with colleagues and from the investment of efforts in other universities.

The discussion so far also indicates a number of tensions that need to be managed if the desirable features of effective self-study described throughout this book are to be realized, and better self-study practice is to be developed. These are illustrated in Table 9.1.

Table 9.1 Self-study: tensions and their resolution

Tension to be managed	Desirable feature to be realized
Internal versus external drivers	Self-study needs to be '*an integral part of the normal process of governing and managing the institution by the governing body and the other bodies within the university responsible for managing its academic and administrative affairs*' (CUC 2002: 9)
Evaluation aimed at audit/ assessment and that aimed at reflection/learning	Self-study should focus on reflection and learning. Otherwise, there is a danger of distorting behaviour and/or doing it only to satisfy external audiences who may have different objectives and values. It must be 'bottom up' and must engage as many staff as possible; universities also need to engage in external discussion about the nature of evidence and external requirements, in order not only to understand these but to help shape them appropriately
Perfecting 'technical' measures and systems at the expense of 'political' sensitivity and staff engagement	Universities need tools that are intelligible and staff to use them intelligently, as well as an appropriate specification for the task. However, there are weaknesses in some of the tools currently available. Universities need to develop their own toolkits to meet their own purposes in the light of their own objectives
Manageability and desirability	Recognition that systems and people have limitations: perfect rationality is not the objective. Resources for self-study need to be proportionate and driven by institutional needs. Supporting staff – to 'do' self-study, understand the outputs or act upon the knowledge gained – is crucial. Clear responsibility for each of these aspects is essential

Addressing the counter-intuitive ▮

J.K. Galbraith wrote in *The Great Crash* (concerning the events of 1929) about the 'failure to know what isn't known' (Galbraith 1954). In 2003 American Secretary of State Donald Rumsfeld won a plain English award for his convoluted attempt to say the same thing. More recently, Slavoj Žižek has added to Rumsfeld's 'known knowns', 'known unknowns' and 'unknown unknowns' what he calls a 'critical fourth category': 'unknown knowns – things which we don't know that we know', or in Freudian terms, 'the knowledge which doesn't know itself' (Žižek 2004). Universities and colleges can fall prey to all of these pathologies. It is highly important to know what we don't know about our performance; it's equally important to be able to accept that from time to time what we think we know is contradicted by the evidence.

So what have we learned from this enormous mass of data, besides the fact that on most hard questions we still do not know enough? Here is a short list of lessons about the University of Brighton which we have found especially salutary:

- although we are relatively secure in financial terms (itself not a bargain, given the state of the sector), we carry a relatively high burden of debt, and are relatively poor at recovering the full costs of research and consultancy;
- 40 per cent of the relatively low group of students who withdraw early from our courses cite 'course not appropriate' as their main reason;
- more of our staff have home obligations that relate to the care of elderly relatives than to child care needs;
- the amount of part-time paid work done by full-time students is not statistically related to their overall financial circumstances;
- part-time students are more concerned about the availability of academic staff outside core hours than the availability of services like libraries and catering;
- the expansion of the proportion of students gaining first and upper second class degrees across the sector has not been matched at the University of Brighton (with negative effects on our league table position – at least until the 2004 *Times* table, when a slight shift resulted in our moving up several places);
- in contrast to the picture at sector level, there is no obvious association between the performance of individual Schools and courses in widening participation on the one hand and 'retention' on the other.

(Appendix 1: Watson 2002)

Conclusions like these serve as significant reality checks. (Another such 'wake-up' call was provided by the Student Union submission to the institutional audit described in Chapter 5.) They also help to achieve what Michael Shattock, writing in the EAIR volume, calls 'resisting fashion' (Shattock 2003b: 62).

The authors and commissioners of the material referred to in this section reflect the wide variety of self-study practitioners introduced in Chapter 3: senior managers; academic and support staff; teachers and researchers; and, on occasions, students and clients. Sometimes, of course, individuals and groups can fall into more than one of these categories. There are clearly many advantages in being able to harness together academic social science, administrative concern, and just the simple inquisitiveness of members of a self-reflective community (see also Yorke 2004). The case study which follows of 'dropout' and retention is a powerful example of the resulting synergy.

Meanwhile, a very important occasional side benefit of team-work is a sense not only of common purpose but also of sympathy: other people's problems are as complex as your own – but not until you understand them. One of the University's chaplains once contributed a workshop to the University's annual Learning and Teaching conference on 'the quality of mercy'. His thesis was that crudely implemented programmes with titles like 'continuous improvement' were not only constructed around a relentless (and merciless) agenda, but were also condemned to end in exhaustion and failure.

Student retention: a case study

Targets and indicators are easier to deal with the higher the level of generality at which they operate. They can become more contentious the further you drill down into the organization, and the more intimate the revelations about variable performance or achievement. The benign term for what is going on here is internal benchmarking. The core challenge is to understand what is going on, to have appropriate expectations and to set appropriate targets for different parts of the organization. The dangers start with stereotyping, scapegoating, and the arrogance of the over-achiever.

Student retention offers a useful case study of some of the difficulties and how this challenge can be addressed – of self-study in action.

Student retention was adopted as the theme of the University of Brighton's Annual Academic Health Process in 2001–02. It led to the decision that more work should be done to put together a statistical picture of what was going on, to identify underlying causes and to suggest possible remedial action to student drop-out. This was despite the fact that the University was then meeting – and has continued to meet – the HEFCE benchmarks for retention (an expected drop-out rate from one year to the next calculated on the basis of the profile of entrants in terms of their qualifications and subject of study). In identifying student retention for this sort of effort, the University recognized that it was an increasingly important issue for the sector (on which HEFCE had indeed been asked to 'bear down' by the then Secretary of State David Blunkett) (Blunkett 2000); that there was a range of performance across the institution; that some areas of rapid growth in student numbers might need additional support to avoid potentially increasing retention difficulties; that it might say something important about the University's provision and support; and of course that it might represent significant personal cost to those individuals who left before completing their course.

The pertinent data are shown in Figures 9.1 and 9.2. Figure 9.1 (for entrants in 2002–03) shows the extent of difference between the retention by the University's Schools and the adjusted sector benchmark (ASB) – a calculation that takes account of the subject of study, and therefore already acknowledges that, nationally, some subjects have higher retention rates than others. In this representation, a School with performance below the ASB is doing better than might be expected since its drop-out rate is *lower*. Figure 9.2 (for entrants in 2000–01) sets the University's performance in the context of the rest of the sector, showing how each university performed relative to its individual benchmarks, highlighting in particular how the University of Brighton stands against some of its chosen comparator group. Again, performance below the ASB means that retention is higher than might be expected. Once again, there are institutions across the range doing significantly better and significantly worse than the ASB would predict. Both sets of data refer to students who were enrolled at the HESES census data but not at the subsequent census date. These two figures illustrate quite starkly the extent of intra- and inter-institutional variation – and indicate at first glance that there may be room for improvement.

In the light of these sorts of data, the Academic Year Review spawned a mass of coordinated effort across the University ranging from better data analysis to some new interventions supported with specific funds in particular Schools and departments seeking to tackle emerging or anticipated retention difficulties. Components of this activity have included:

- analysis of data about successive cohorts of degree entrants from

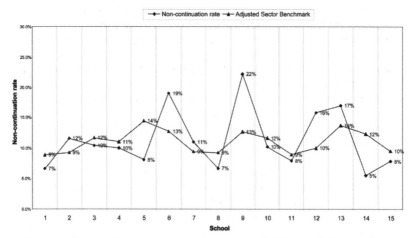

Figure 9.1 Overall non-continuation rates of 2002–03 full-time first degree entrants: University of Brighton Schools vs adjusted sector benchmarks

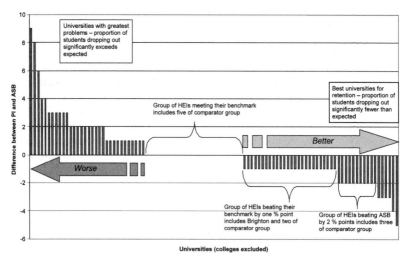

Figure 9.2 Universities and their expected retention performance

1999–2000 onwards, at School level, leading to a report circulated to Deans, Heads of Schools and major University committees;
- a postal questionnaire to students who have left early asking them more about their reasons for so doing and circulation to Heads of any responses of particular concern about their Schools;

- a review within Schools of the reasons offered by students when notifying the School of their intention to leave early;
- a requirement of Heads of School to comment on the retention data pertaining to their School;
- preparation of a good practice template derived from national reports and comparison between university practice and the template, identifying gaps in practice and also local good practice that could be shared across the institution;
- sponsorship of a number of School-level intervention projects, three of which appear to have had an impact on retention rates in those Schools –
  - supporting intending and first-year students with student ambassadors/mentors in a School with a higher than average withdrawal rate in its first semester;
  - supporting first-year students in a rapidly growing School showing some indications of emerging retention problems with a new single point-of-contact Student Advice and Guidance Tutor;
  - supporting a cohort of non-traditional distance learners on a new course with additional e-learning access, materials and staff back-up to the 'e-support';
- a new student transition project run by Student Services to assist all new students to make the transition to higher education;
- discussion of the data, implications and practice at a pair of senior staff seminars (for Deans, Heads and the Senior Management Team) facilitated by an external expert;
- setting up the Student Retention Review Group, which brings together representatives of relevant services, those involved in specific projects and learning and teaching developments, and senior academics;
- launching an annual conference series to focus attention and share good practice; and
- institutional involvement in a national Fund for the Development of Teaching and Learning (FDTL) centre-led project looking at student retention in the biological sciences.

This case study exemplifies the intimate relationship between the data cycle, the quality cycle and the planning cycle, with data analysis informing reflection on practice and resource decisions. Thus, the University's qualitative interventions on retention reflect decisions taken during the planning cycle, prompted by a concern emerging during a previous quality cycle, and underpinned by increasingly sophisticated quantitative and qualitative self-knowledge at the heart of the data cycle.

We have tried neither to be simplistic, nor to assume that the object is to hold on to every student who enrols. As Liston notes of managing quality:

> organisations which apply quality management principles and practices use data and information widely and wisely. Key performance measures for processes and outcomes are identified and measured. Statistical and charting techniques … are used at all levels for decision-making and reporting. Decisions are made on sound evidence, not gut reactions. Actions are based on knowledge and understanding, together with sensible and sensitive application of measurement in context – and with an acceptance of the value of diversity.
>
> (Liston 1999: 67)

Some of the findings are instructive in themselves and some point strongly to the need for further data and investigation, both within the University and nationally. Here are some of the statistically significant findings for the 2002–03 cohort:

- mature entrants are more likely to withdraw than young entrants;
- male students are more likely to withdraw than female students, but in some Schools there is a pronounced opposite effect;
- ethnicity and disability do not appear to be factors in rates of withdrawal;
- overseas students are more likely to withdraw and in some Schools this is markedly so;
- entry qualifications have a non-linear relationship on withdrawal rates, under the new UCAS system, compared to previous years where there was a clear linear relationship;
- accommodation in a hall of residence appears to reduce the likelihood of withdrawal significantly, especially for young male students.

(Appendix 1 2004c)

The University has also been concerned to listen to the students concerned and try to find out why they have chosen to leave. Students are interviewed informally when they let their School know that they want to leave, and this is followed up by either a postal or telephone survey. This more qualitative research about students' reasons for leaving the University shows the weight attached to the match between expectations and experience as well as to balancing the various elements of contemporary student life (Appendix 1 2004g). Table 9.2 shows the range of factors influencing a decision to withdraw and Table 9.3 shows the main reasons given for their decision by those departing early in 2002–03. It is clear from these data that many individual decisions, and the statistical patterns that emerge, reflect complex mixtures of the academic, personal, social and financial. The University has only limited purchase on some of these. The complexity of the picture from these data is supported by the findings from an investigation by three of the Schools undertaking specific retention projects described above. Taken together, they indicate the importance of students' development of social bonds as a factor in preventing withdrawal. This is a subtle message for any institution – it is not about University-sponsored partying, but about what can be done more systematically to support a feeling of belonging, with access to those who can assist this, whether staff or other students. The intervention projects are therefore largely about work to bolster the ease with which students can do this, whether with additional access to learning and peer support, or through existing students acting as mentors to those about to or newly joining the institution.

Table 9.2 University of Brighton: results of postal questionnaire to students withdrawing from their courses, 2002–03

Factor affecting withdrawal	Substantial influence	Some influence	No influence
Course content not what I expected	35 (23)	38 (25)	81 (53)
I chose the wrong field of study	24 (16)	21(14)	108 (71)
The pace or workload was too great	11 (7)	42 (27)	100 (65)
I was experiencing financial difficulties as a result of my studies	16 (11)	24 (16)	108 (73)
I was dissatisfied by the quality of teaching	21 (14)	22 (14)	109 (72)
It was hard to balance paid work commitments with my studies	32 (21)	26 (17)	96 (62)

Note: Data indicate number and percentage () of respondents, 170 responses

The hard part starts once you have gathered this sort of information and gained a better feel for student perceptions as well as for the aggregate data. It is likely to lead to decisions about resources and

Table 9.3 University of Brighton: main reasons for student withdrawal, 2002–03

What was your main reason for withdrawal?	Number	%
The course content was not what I expected	19	12
I chose the wrong field of study	14	9
I was unable to continue because of personal illness/injury	14	9
It was hard to balance paid work commitments with my studies	13	8
I was dissatisfied with the quality of teaching	12	8
I was not suited to the profession linked to my course	12	8

Note: 157 responses

about necessary or desirable changes in practice – as well as about doing more research. For example, at Brighton, we are now changing our structures to support students who want to change direction within the University; doing more research into the needs of part-time students, where the national data offer little help; and including explicit consideration of the School-level data in the Annual Academic Health Process, in order to make this part of regular and established quality assessment and enhancement.

Facing the future

To take a more homely perspective, and in addition to attempting to assess the state of the art in higher educational self-study, the material in this book has been revealing (we hope) about the condition of the University of Brighton. We hope that we have also explained some of the dilemmas of institutional management in a sector that is capable of wild fluctuations in direction and priorities. Indeed, at times, institutional leadership can be tempted by George Orwell's injunction in his essay of 1940, *Inside the Whale* (he was writing about the 'quietism' in the novels of Henry Miller):

> Get inside the whale – or rather, admit that you are inside the whale (for you *are*, of course). Give yourself over to the world-process, stop fighting against it or pretending that you control it; simply accept it, endure it, record it.
>
> (Orwell 1940)

For universities and colleges in the UK, the voyage of the whale is hugely dependent upon the vagaries of national policy – more, we would suggest, than in any advanced society whose higher education system is known to us. In this sense, the kind of scoping set out in Chapter 7 – the external face of institutional self-study – is a critical element of corporate well-being.

As for the plethora of exercises described throughout this book, they necessarily represent a snapshot of activity, and the currency of the empirical data will degrade fast. The principal lessons are of three types, relating to the following questions, and we conclude by proposing these as a readily generalizable set of motives for intelligent self-study.

- How are we doing, in both absolute and comparative terms?
- Is what we are doing right, in terms of institutional security and strength of purpose in difficult times?
- Is what we are doing the best it can be, or (to put the question more calmly) can we do it better?

The short answers to these questions, in sequence, are: 'not badly', 'apparently so', and 'we wish we knew more'. Question three is in fact the holy grail of institutional self-study: without aspiring to answer it, the other activity seems fairly pointless.

Crucially, we have emphasized some of the softer and more cultural sides of the university as a community. These too can be formally tested. In 2003, the University took part in an exercise designed to investigate its 'organizational character'. This was in the context of a programme of senior management development, covering about sixty of the University's academic and administrative leaders. It was based on an instrument designed and copyrighted by Azure Consulting International, and applied by the consultants TMP. The results mirror many of the more fine-grained conclusions derived from the mass of information described throughout this book. Our top-level results are set out in Figure 9.3 (Appendix 1: Azure Consulting International 2003).

As can be readily seen, the University of Brighton scores high on indices relating to integrity and resilience, but lower on its self-perception of distinctiveness, flexibility and readiness for change. Clearly more self-study is required.

If there is a single maxim which sums up the arguments we have tried to make in the book, it goes as follows: try to align what you have to do with what you want to do.

Universities and colleges have been very good at managing this particular tension throughout their long and adaptable history. For

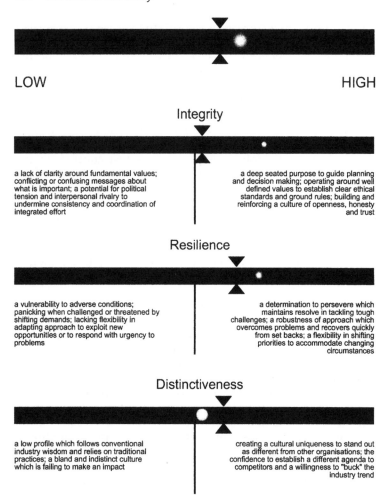

Figure 9.3 University of Brighton: organizational character

Note: △ = organizational benchmark; ○ = University of Brighton

Source: Appendix 1: Azure Consulting International (2003)

centuries they have been peculiarly adept at managing both continuity and change; at sponsoring both conservation and innovation; and at bowing to the inevitable while constructing the circumstances in which the inevitable can be turned to unlikely advantage. To paraphrase Marx, they have succeeded in making their own history while understanding that, in doing so, the circumstances are not of their choosing. One of the strongest contemporary accounts of what this means for the academy is supplied by Donald Kennedy, former President of Stanford, in his book *Academic Duty*:

> Universities are in a dynamic equilibrium with society. On the one hand, they appear to lag behind it, acting as conservators of its history and archivists of its highest cultural attainments. On the other hand, they are seen as leaders, adventuring into new knowledge domains, developing transforming technologies, and serving as the seedbed for novel and often disturbing ideas.
>
> Both these roles are part of the university's academic duty.
> (Kennedy 1997: 265)

In an era when, as we have shown, the academic community is increasingly compelled to act in partnership with others, and to manage another tension – between competition and collaboration – self-study can also help to identify who its real stakeholders are. This involves getting behind the rhetoric about so-called stakeholding: to be a stakeholder, you have to have invested something, to share the risk; otherwise you will fulfil the old public sector manager's stereotype – of a stakeholder as 'someone who can do you harm'. Some of the more extreme spokespersons from business or politics frequently fail this test.

It is also possible for governments to speak with forked tongue. For example, in mid-2004 the UK's Department for Education and Skills (DfES) published a much vaunted 'five year strategy', part of a Whitehall sequence about 'putting people at the heart of public services'. In his introduction, the Secretary of State talks about the conditions of achieving 'excellence'. One such is apparently professional autonomy: 'the people our whole system depends upon – those at the front line – must be given the freedom to shape and reshape the offer [*sic*] to meet different and changing needs'. He concludes by saying: 'and it depends on Ministers like me holding our nerve and being able to resist the lure of the next initiative in favour of a system that drives its own improvement more and more' (DfES 2004a: 4–5).

This is, of course, not how it feels. The chapter on higher education is full of assertions which are themselves lacking any basis in evidence. We have alluded to some of these above. Another example is the following: 'teaching quality is still too variable; and we need to make sure, especially with the introduction of variable fees, that all students are getting a good deal from their university teaching' (DfES 2004a: 92). In fact, quality assessment has shown teaching quality to be remarkably consistent, while the case has just not been made that variable income will achieve reduced variability in the quality of teaching (it seems unlikely). Meanwhile, the lure of the 'next initiative' is just too powerful. The chapter is silent on the Department's subsequent announcement of decisions to relax arrangements for university title and degree-awarding powers, to allow for a UK-based 'for profit' sector and to break the link between teaching and research (DfES 2004b).

In such a complex and contingent arena, self-study is a vital solvent. It combines the two essential injunctions: not just 'know thyself', but also 'know what is really going on'. Both injunctions operate against rapidly moving targets.

- The questions will change. Hot questions at the moment include the DfES impatience at the apparent lack of progress on the social composition of HEIs (although, as we have shown, by international comparison the UK is doing rather well). This can be contrasted with the Treasury and DTI's rather longer horizon on the question of university support for science and innovation. Why can we not have a ten-year strategy for both?
- The stakeholders will change. All around the world universities and colleges are coming to terms with the dramatic increase in mutual dependence between higher education and health. When they are not working for their own renewal, universities have always served other clients. Health is the latest and the most potentially intrusive. In the UK, the Longer Term Strategy Group of UUK has established that 16 per cent of all fee income and 30 per cent of all research support is related to medicine, health and social care (UUK 2004).
- The academic community itself will change. As we hope we have demonstrated, students and other clients of the university, as well as all of the categories of staff in higher education, will continue to bring different interests, capabilities and needs into the community. This is especially as a consequence of developments in Information and Communications Technologies and the increasing impact of global markets, communications and sensibilities.

At the end of the day, knowledge is always a kind of power, however partial, incomplete or provisional it may be. Sound institutional self-study should answer some questions and ask some others; it should validate some opinions and unsettle some others; it should reassure and it should challenge. It should help us all to face the future as responsibly and effectively as we can.

REFERENCES

ACU (Association of Commonwealth Universities) (2001) *Engagement as a Core Value for the University: A Consultation Document*. London: ACU.

Ahier, J., Beck, J. and Moore, R. (2002) *Graduate Citizens? Issues of Citizenship and Higher Education*. London: Routledge Falmer.

Antony, J. and Preece, D. (eds.) (2002) *Understanding, Managing and Implementing Quality – Frameworks, Techniques and Cases*. London: Routledge.

Argyris, C. (1999) *On Organisational Learning*, 2nd edn. Oxford: Blackwell.

AUCC (Association of Universities and Colleges of Canada) (2002) *Trends in Higher Education*. Ottawa: AUCC.

Balanced Scorecard Institute (2004) *What is the Balanced Scorecard?* (http://www.balancedscorecard.org). Downloaded 14 July 2004.

Barkers (2001) *The Binary Line Revisited*. London: Barkers.

Barkers (2003) *The Relevance of Reputation: Reputation and Branding in University Choice*. London: Barkers.

Barnett, R. (1992) *Improving Higher Education: Total Quality Care*. Buckingham: Society for Research into Higher Education and Open University Press.

Barnett, R. (1994) Power, enlightenment and quality evaluation. *European Journal of Education*, 29(2): 165–79.

Begg, R. (ed.) (2003) *The Dialogue between Higher Education Research and Practice*. Dordrecht, Boston and London: Kluwer Academic Publishers.

Blunkett, D.(2000) Higher Education Funding for 2001–02 and Beyond. Letter received by Sir Michael Checkland, Chair of Higher Education Funding Council for England, 29 November.

BNQP (Baldrige National Quality Program) (2004) *Education Criteria for Performance Excellence*. Gaithersburg, MD: National Institute of Standards and Technology.

Borden, V.M.H. and Banta, T.W. (eds) (1994) *Using Performance Indicators to Guide Strategic Decision Making*, New Directions for Institutional Research 82(2). San Francisco, CA: Jossey-Bass.

Borden, V.M.H. and Botrill, K.V. (1994) Performance indicators: history, definitions and methods, in Borden, V.M.H. and Banta, T.W. (eds.) *Using Performance Indicators to Guide Strategic Decision Making*, New Directions for Institutional Research 82(2). San Francisco, CA: Jossey-Bass.

Borden, V.M.H. and Owens, J.L.Z. (2001) *Measuring Quality: Choosing Among Surveys and Other Assessments of College Quality*. Washington, DC: American Council on Education Center for Policy Analysis and Association for Institutional Research.

Bourner, T., Bowden, R. and Laing, S. (2000) *Professional Doctorates: The Development of Professional Doctorates in England in the 1990s*. Brighton: University of Brighton Education Research Centre Occasional Paper.

Bowden, R. (2000) Fantasy higher education: university and college league tables. *Quality in Higher Education*, 6(1): 41–60.

Brennan, J. and Shah, T. (2000) *Managing Quality in Higher Education – An International Perspective on Institutional Assessment and Change*. Buckingham and Philadelphia: OECD, Society for Research into Higher Education and Open University Press.

Brennan, J. and Williams, R. (2004) *Collecting and Using Student Feedback: A Guide to Good Practice*. York: Learning and Teaching Support Network (LTSN). (http://www.hefce.ac.uk/Pubs/RDreports/2002/rd15_02/). Downloaded 26 July 2004.

Brighton and Hove City Council (1999) *Scenario Planning*. Unpublished.

Browning, G. (2004) *How to . . . know yourself*. Guardian Weekend, 17 April.

BRRG (Better Regulation Review Group) (2003) *Interim Report*. (www.hero.ac.uk/images/pdfs/23396.pdf). Downloaded 28 July 2004.

Burke, J.C., Minassians, H. and Young, P. (2002) State performance reporting indicators: do they work? *Planning for Higher Education*, 31(1): 15–29.

Bushaway, R.W. (2003) *Managing Research*. Maidenhead and Philadelphia, PA: Open University Press.

Bynner, J., Dolton, P., Feinstein, L., Makepiece, G., Malmberg, L. and Woods, L. (2003) *Revisiting the Benefits of Higher Education. A Report by the Bedford Group for Lifecourse and Statistical Studies, Institute of Education*. Bristol: HEFCE.

Cabinet Office, Centre for Management and Policy Studies (undated) *Public Sector Excellence Programme Support Pack*. Downloaded 28 July 2004 from www.cmps.gov.uk/performance/tools/efqm/model/publicsector.asp

Cabinet Office, Performance and Innovation Unit (undated) *The Future and How to Think About It*. Downloaded 28 July 2004 from www.number 10.gov.uk/su/future/future/shtml

Cabinet Office, Performance and Innovation Unit (2001a) *Benchmarking UK Strategic Futures Work*. Downloaded 28 July 2004 from www.strategy.gov.uk.output.page3769.asp

Cabinet Office, Performance and Innovation Unit (2001b) *A Futurist's Toolbox – Methodologies in Future Work*. Downloaded 28 July 2004 from www.strategy.gov.uk/output/page3769.asp

Cabinet Office, Performance and Innovation Unit (2001c) *Understanding Best Practice in Strategic Futures Work*. Downloaded 28 July 2004 from www.strategy.gov.uk.output.page3769.asp

Cave, M., Hanney, S., Henkel, M. and Kogan, M. (1997) *The Use of Performance*

Indicators in Higher Education – The Challenge of the Quality Movement, 3rd edn. London: Jessica Kingsley.

Chan, S.S. (1993) Changing roles of institutional research in strategic management. *Research in Higher Education,* 34 (5): 533–49.

Chapleo, C. (2003) *Standing Out From The Crowd.* St Albans: Communications Management.

Choo, C.W. (1998) *The Knowing Organization.* Oxford: Oxford University Press.

CIHE (Council for Industry and Higher Education) (2004) *Higher Education and the Public Good: A Contribution to the Debate.* London: CIHE.

CIHE (Council for Industry and Higher Education) and AIM (Advanced Institute of Management Research) (2004) *Solving the Skills Gap.* London: CIHE.

CUC (Committee of University Chairmen) (2002) *Interim Report of the Working Party on the Review of Institutional Performance.* (http://www.sheffield.ac.uk/cuc/pubs/interim.pdf). Downloaded 28 July 2004

Cuthbert, R. (2003) 'Students – Customers, Citizens and the Chattering Classes'. Introductory workshop paper for the AUA Corporate Planning Forum Conference, November (unpublished).

Davenport, T.H. and Prusak, L. (2000) *Working Knowledge – How Organizations Manage What They Know.* Boston, MA: Harvard Business School Press.

Daxner, M. (2002) *Universities as Sites of Citizenship* (mimeo).

DfES (Department for Education and Skills) (2003) *The Future of Higher Education.* London: The Stationery Office.

DfES (2004a) *Five Year Strategy for Children and Learners.* London: The Stationery Office.

DfES (2004b) *Final decision on degree awarding powers and use of university title.* Press Notice, 16 July. (www.dfes.gov.uk/pns/DisplayPN.cgi?pn_ id=2004_0139). Downloaded 29 July 2004.

Dill, D. (1998) Evaluating the 'evaluative state': implications for research in higher education. *European Journal of Education,* 33(3).

Dyson, R.G. and O'Brien, F.A. (eds.) (1998) *Strategic Development.* Chichester: John Wiley.

Duke, C. (2002) *Managing the Learning University.* Buckingham and Philadelphia: Society for Research into Higher Education and Open University Press.

Education Guardian (2003) Don your way, 25 November.

EFQM (European Framework for Quality Management) (2002) *EQFM Excellence Model. Public and Voluntary Sector Version.* Brussels: EFQM.

Ehrenberg, R.G. (1999) Adam Smith Goes to College: an economist becomes an academic administrator. *Journal of Economic Perspectives,* 13(1): 99–116.

Elkin, J. and Law, D. (eds.) (2000) *Managing Information.* Buckingham: Open University Press.

ESRC (Economic and Social Research Council), and OST (Office for Science and Technology) (1999) *Britain Towards 2010: The Changing Business Environment.* London: HMSO.

EUA (European University Association) (2004) *10 Year Anniversary Institutional Evaluation Programme.* Brussels: EUA.

EUA/ACE (European University Association/American Council on Education)

(2002) *The Brave (and Smaller) New World of Higher Education: A Transatlantic View*. Washington, DC: ACE.

European Commission, Forward Studies Unit (1999) *Scenarios Europe 2010*. Brussels: European Commission.

Fielden, J. (2003) Internationalising higher education, in *Commonwealth Education Partnerships* 2003. London: The Stationery Office.

Fielden, J. and Carr, M. (2000) CHEMS International Benchmarking Club, in N. Jackson and H. Lund (eds.) *Benchmarking for Higher Education*. Buckingham: Society for Research into Higher Education and Open University Press.

Florida, R. (2002) *The Rise of the Creative Class, and How It's Transforming Work, Leisure, Community and Creative Life*. New York, NY: Basic Books.

Frand, J.L. (2000) The information age mindset; changes in students and implications for higher education. *Educause Review*, 35(5): 14–25.

Fuller, S. (2002) *Knowledge Management Foundations*. Boston, MA: Butterworth-Heinemann.

Galbraith, J.K. (1954) *The Great Crash*. Boston, MA: Houghton Mifflin.

Garratt, B. (2001) *The Learning Organization – Developing Democracy at Work*. London: HarperCollins.

Gater, D.S. (2002) *A Review of Measures Used in* US News and World Report's *'America's Best Colleges'*. Gainesville, FL: Lombardi Program on Measuring University Performance, University of Florida. (http://thecenter.ufl.edu/Gater0702.pdf). Downloaded 28 July 2004.

Geal, V., Harvey, L. and Moon, S. (1997) The United Kingdom institutional self-evaluation and quality, in H.A. Strydom, L.O.K. Lategan and A. Muller (eds.) *Enhancing Institutional Self-Evaluation and Quality in South African Higher Education: National and International Perspectives*. Bloemfontein: University of the Orange Free State.

Gibbons, M., Limoges, C., Nowotny, H., Schwarzman, S., Scott, P. and Trow, M. (1994) *The New Production of Knowledge: The Dynamics of Science and Research in Contemporary Societies*. London: Sage Publications.

Goddard, J., Charles, D., Pike, A., Potts, G. and Bradley, D. (1994) *Universities and Communities*. London: Committee of Vice-Chancellors and Principals.

Greatrix, P. (2003) *How to Read League Tables*. Cheltenham: UCAS.

Gumport, P.J., Cappelli, P., Massy, W.F., Nettles, M.T., Petersen, M.W., Shavelson, R.J. and Zemsky, R. (2002) *Beyond Dead Reckoning: Research Priorities for Redirecting American Higher Education*. Stanford, CA: National Center for Postsecondary Improvement. Reprinted by CHERI (Centre for Higher Education Research and Information) (2003), London.

Haynes, P., Ip, K., Saintas, P., Stanier, S., Palmer, H., Thomas, N. *et al.* (2004) Responding to technological change – IT skills and the academic teaching profession. *Active Learning in Higher Education*, 5 (2): 152–65.

HEFCE (Higher Education Funding Council for England) (1999) *Performance Indicators in Higher Education*, 1996–97, 1997–98. Bristol: HEFCE.

HEFCE (2001a) *Risk Management: A Guide to Good Practice for Higher Education Institutions*. Bristol: HEFCE.

HEFCE (2001b) *Strategies for Widening Participation in Higher Education. A Guide to Good Practice*. Bristol: HEFCE.

HEFCE (2001c) *Strategies for Learning and Teaching in Higher Education: A Guide to Good Practice.* Bristol: HEFCE.

HEFCE (2001d) *Analysis of Strategies for Learning and Teaching: Research Report by Professor Graham Gibbs.* Bristol: HEFCE.

HEFCE (2001e) *Wider Benefits of Higher Education.* Bristol: HEFCE.

HEFCE (2002a) *Rewarding and Developing Staff in Higher Education: Good Practice in Setting HR Strategies.* Bristol: HEFCE.

HEFCE (2002b) *Information on Quality and Standards in Higher Education. Final Report of the Task Group.* Bristol: HEFCE.

HEFCE (2002c) *Evaluating the Regional Contribution of an HEI. A Benchmarking Approach.* Bristol: HEFCE.

HEFCE (2002d) *Financial Strategy in Higher Education Institutions.* Bristol: HEFCE.

HEFCE (2002e) *Academic Staff: Trends and Projections.* Bristol: HEFCE.

HEFCE (2002f) *Estates Management Statistics.* Bristol: HEFCE.

HEFCE (2003a) *Investment Decision Making. A Guide to Good Practice.* Bristol: HEFCE.

HEFCE (2003b) *Energy Management in Higher Education. Value for Money Study.* Bristol: HEFCE.

HEFCE (2003c) *Catering Management in Higher Education: National Report and Toolchest.* Bristol: HEFCE.

HEFCE (2003d) *Implementing HR Strategies: A Guide to Good Practice.* Bristol: HEFCE.

HEFCE (2003e) *Report of the Teaching Quality Information Pilot Project* (John Slater). Bristol: HEFCE.

HEFCE (2003f) *Information on Quality and Standards in Higher Education.* Final guidance. Bristol: HEFCE.

HEFCE (2004a) *Higher Education Business Interaction Survey 2001–02.* Bristol: HEFCE.

HEFCE (2004b) *Recurrent Grants for 2004–05.* Bristol: HEFCE.

HEFCE (2004c) *HEFCE Strategic Plan 2003–08* (Revised April 2004). Bristol: HEFCE.

HEFCE (2004d) *National Student Survey 2005: Consultation.* Bristol: HEFCE.

HEPI (Higher Education Policy Institute) (2003) *Higher Education Supply and Demand to 2010.* (www.hepi.ac.uk/articles/docs/demand.doc). Downloaded 26 July 2004.

HEQC (Higher Education Quality Council) (1997) *Managing Quality and Standards in UK Higher Education – Approaches to Self-Evaluation and Self-Regulation.* London: HEQC.

HESA (Higher Education Statistics Agency) (2003) *Data Analysis.* (http://www.hesa.ac.uk/about/home.htm). Downloaded 28 July 2004.

Heywood, J. (2000) *Assessment in Higher Education.* London: Jessica Kingsley.

HMT (HM Treasury) (2003) *Lambert Review of Business–University Collaboration.* London: HM Treasury.

HMT (2004) *Science and Innovation Framework 2004–2014.* London: The Stationery Office.

Hodgkinson, G.P. and Sparrow, P.R. (2002) *The Competent Organization.* Buckingham: Open University Press.

Howard, R. (ed.) (2001) *Institutional Research: Decision Support in Higher Education*. Tallahassee, FL: Association for Institutional Research.

IBE (Institute of Business Ethics) (2001) *Risky Business: Towards Best Practice in Managing Reputation Risk*. London: IBE.

Jackson, N. (1997) The role of evaluation in self-regulating higher education institutions, in *Managing Quality and Standards in UK Higher Education – Approaches to Self-Evaluation and Self-Regulation*. London: HEQC.

Jackson, N. (2002) *Benchmarking in UK HE: An Overview*. (http://www.ltsn.ac. uk/application.asp?section=generic&app=resources.asp&process=full_record &id=151). Downloaded 20 July 2004.

Jackson, N. (2003) *Developing a Network for Institutional Researchers: Working Paper 1*. (www.ltsn.ac.uk/application.asp?app=resources.asp&process=full_ record&section=generic&id=150). Downloaded 26 July 2004.

Jackson, N. and Lund, H. (2000) Benchmarking for higher education: taking stock, in N. Jackson and H. Lund (eds) *Benchmarking for Higher Education*. Buckingham: Society for Research into Higher Education and Open University Press.

Jackson, N. and Lund, H. (eds.) (2000) *Benchmarking for Higher Education*. Buckingham: Society for Research into Higher Education and Open University Press.

Jamieson, D.M. (1988) Self-study and its role in strategic planning, in H.R. Kells and F.A. van Vught (eds.) *Self-Regulation, Self-Study and Program Review in Higher Education*. Culemborg, Netherlands: Lemma.

Jarratt Committee (1985) *Report of the Steering Committee for Efficiency Studies in Universities*. London: Committee of Vice-Chancellors and Principals.

Johnes, J. and Taylor, J. (1990) *Performance Indicators in Higher Education*. Buckingham: Society for Research into Higher Education and Open University Press.

Kaplan, R.S. and Norton, D.P (1992) The balanced scorecard – measures that drive performance. *Harvard Business Review*, January–February. Reprinted in Dyson, R.G and O'Brien, F.A. (eds.) (1998) *Strategic Development: Methods and Models*. Chichester: Wiley.

Kay, J. (2003) *The Truth about Markets: Their Genius, Their Limits, Their Follies*. London: Allen Lane.

Keep, E. and Rainbird, H. (2002) Towards the learning organization?, in F. Reeve, M. Cartwright and R. Edwards (eds) *Supporting Lifelong Learning. Volume 2: Organizing Learning*. London: Routledge Falmer.

Kells, H.R. (1992) *Self-Regulation in Higher Education – A Multi-National Perspective on Collaborative Systems of Quality Assurance and Control*. London: Jessica Kingsley.

Kells, H.R. (1995) *Self-Study Processes: A Guide to Self-Evaluation in Higher Education*, 4th edn. Phoenix, AZ: Orynx Press.

Kells, H.R. and van Vught, F.A. (eds.) (1988) *Self-Regulation, Self-Study and Program Review in Higher Education*. Culemborg, Netherlands: Lemma.

Kelly, U., Marsh, R. and McNicoll, I. (2002) *The Impact of Higher Education Institutions on the UK Economy. A Report for Universities UK*. London: UUK.

Kennedy, D. (1997) *Academic Duty*. Cambridge, MA: Harvard University Press.

Kidd, J.B. (2002) Knowledge creation in Japanese manufacturing companies in

Italy: reflections upon organizational learning, in F. Reeve, M. Cartwright and R. Edwards (eds.) *Supporting Lifelong Learning. Volume 2: Organizing Learning*. London: Routledge Falmer.

King, D. (2002) 'Science policy in government'. Marie Jahoda Lecture, University of Sussex, 9 October.

Knight, W.E. (ed.) (2003) *The Primer for Institutional Research*. Tallahassee, FL: Association for Institutional Research.

Kogan, M. (ed.) (1989) *Evaluating Higher Education*. London: Jessica Kingsley.

Kumar, A. and Douglas, C. (2002) Self-assessment frameworks for business organizations, in J. Antony and D. Preece (eds) *Understanding, Managing and Implementing Quality – Frameworks, Techniques and Cases*. London: Routledge.

Lippmann, W. (1914, 1961) *Drift and Mastery*. Englewood Cliffs, NJ: Prentice-Hall.

Liston, C. (1999) *Managing Quality and Standards*. Buckingham and Philadelphia, PA: Open University Press.

Little, S., Quintas, P. and Ray, T. (eds.) (2002) *Managing Knowledge: An Essential Reader*. London: Sage Publications.

Lombardi, J.V. (2000) *University Improvement: The Permanent Challenge*. (http://thecenter.ufl.edu/socarolina3.htm). Downloaded 28 July 2004

McNicoll, I., McCluskey, K. and Kelly, U. (1997) *The Impact of Universities and Colleges on the UK Economy*. London: CVCP.

Malcolm, J. and Zukacs, M. (2001) Bridging pedagogic gaps: conceptual discontinuities in higher education. *Teaching in Higher Education*, 6(1): 33–42.

Miles, R.E., Snow, C.C., Matthews, J.A., Miles, G. and Coleman H.J. (2002) Organizing in the knowledge age: anticipating the cellular form, in S. Little, P. Quintas and T. Ray (eds.) *Managing Knowledge: An Essential Reader*. London: Sage Publications.

Milner, E.M. (2000) *Managing Information and Knowledge in the Public Sector*. London: Routledge.

Mintzberg, H. (2000) *The Rise and Fall of Strategic Planning*. Harlow: Pearson Education Limited.

Mintzberg, H., Ahlstrand, B. and Lampel, J. (1998) *Strategy Safari*. Harlow: Pearson Education Limited.

NCE (National Commission on Education) (2003) *Learning to Succeed. The Next Decade*. The National Commission on Education Follow-Up Group. Brighton: University of Brighton Education Research Centre Occasional Paper.

NCIHE (National Committee of Inquiry into Higher Education) (1997) *Higher Education in the Learning Age*. London: HMSO.

Neave, G. (1998) The evaluative state reconsidered. *European Journal of Education*, 33(3).

Neave, G. (2003) Institutional research: from case study to strategic instrument, in R. Begg (ed.) *The Dialogue Between Higher Education Research and Practice*. Dordrecht, London and Boston, MA: Kluwer Academic Publishers.

Nedwek, B.P. and Neal, J.E. (1994) Performance indicators and rational management tools: a comparative assessment of projects in North America and Europe. *Research in Higher Education*, 35(1): 75–103.

NIST (National Institute of Standards and Technology) (2002) *Baldrige Award Winners Beat the S and P for Eighth Year.* Press release, 7 March. (http://www.nist.gov/public_affairs/releases/g02–11.htm). Downloaded 28 July 2004.

Nonaka, I. and Takeuchi, H. (1995) *The Knowledge-Creating Company: How Japanese Companies Create the Dynamics of Innovation.* New York, NY: Oxford University Press.

Nuffield Trust (2003) *Involving People in Public Disclosure of Clinical Data: Report on Research with User Organisations and Patients.* London: Nuffield Trust.

O'Brien, F.A. (2002) 'Scenario Planning'. Presentation for Warwick Business School (unpublished).

O'Donovan, J. (2000) The administrator and information, in J. Elkin and D. Law (eds.) *Managing Information.* Buckingham: Open University Press.

OECD IMHE-HEFCE (Organisation for Economic Cooperation and Development Institutional Management in Higher Education – Higher Education Funding Council for England) (2004) *International Comparative Higher Education Financial Management and Governance Project. Financial Management and Governance in HEIs: England.* Bristol: HEFCE. (http://www.hefce.ac.uk/Pubs/RDreports/2004/rd01_04/). Downloaded 25 July 2004.

OPM (Office for Public Management) (2002) *Development of HR Strategies: Learning from Assessing Strategies and Advising Institutions. A Report to the HEFCE by the Office for Public Management.* Bristol: HEFCE. (http://www.hefce.ac.uk/Pubs/RDreports/2002/rd15_02/). Downloaded 25 July 2004.

Orwell, G. (1940) Inside the whale, in S. Orwell and I. Angus *The Collected Essays, Journalism and Letters of George Orwell. Vol. 1: An Age Like This.* Harmondsworth: Penguin (1970).

PA Consulting (2004a) *Survival of the Fittest: A Survey of the Leadership of Strategic Change in Higher Education.* London: PA Consulting Group.

PA Consulting (2004b) *Better Accountability Revisited: Review of Accountability Costs 2004. A Report to HEFCE by PA Consulting.* London: PA Consulting. (http://www.hefce.ac.uk/Pubs/RDreports/2004/rd06_04/). Downloaded 25 July 2004.

Pettigrew, A. and Whipp, R. (1991) *Managing Change for Competitive Success.* Oxford: Blackwell.

Pike, G.R. (2004) Measuring quality: a comparison of US news rankings and NSSE benchmarks. *Research in Higher Education*, 45(2): 193–208.

Power, M. (1999) *The Audit Society: Rituals of Verification.* Oxford: Oxford University Press.

QAA (Quality Assurance Agency) for Higher Education (2002a) *Evaluation of Academic Review in Wales 2002.* (www.qaa.ac.uk/revreps/welsh_evalreport_wales_intro.htm). Downloaded 30 July 2004.

QAA (2002b) *Handbook for Institutional Audit: England.* Gloucester: QAA.

QAA (2003a) *Institutional Audit: England – Key Features and Findings of the First Audits.* Gloucester: QAA.

QAA (2003b) *Handbook for Enhancement-led Institutional Review: Scotland.* Gloucester: QAA.

QAA (2003c) *Institutional Audit Report: Institute of Education, University of London*, March. Gloucester: QAA

QAA (2003d) *Institutional Audit Report: London Business School*, May. Gloucester: QAA.

QAA (2003e) *Institutional Audit Report: Middlesex University*, March. Gloucester: QAA.

QAA (2003f) *Institutional Audit Report: Royal Academy of Music*, March. Gloucester: QAA.

QAA (2003g) *Institutional Audit Report: Royal College of Art*, March. Gloucester: QAA.

QAA (2003h) *Institutional Audit Report: Royal Northern College of Music*; May. Gloucester: QAA.

QAA (2003i) *Institutional Audit Report: School of Oriental and African Studies, University of London*, April. Gloucester: QAA.

QAA (2003j) *Institutional Audit Report: University of Bradford*, November. Gloucester: QAA.

QAA (2003k) *Institutional Audit Report: University of Cambridge*, April. Gloucester: QAA.

QAA (2003l) *Institutional Audit Report: University of Essex*, November. Gloucester: QAA.

QAA (2003m) *Institutional Audit Report: University of Lincoln*, May. Gloucester: QAA.

QAA (2003n) *Institutional Audit Report: University of Sheffield*, November. Gloucester: QAA.

QAA (2003o) *Institutional Audit Report: University of Southampton*, December. Gloucester: QAA.

QAA (2003p) *Institutional Audit Report: University of York*, December. Gloucester: QAA.

QAA (2004) *Institutional Audit Report: University of Liverpool*, February. Gloucester: QAA.

Raban, C. and Turner, E. (2003) *Academic Risk – HEFCE Good Management Practice Project, Quality Risk Management in Higher Education*. Bristol: HEFCE.

Ramsden, B. (2003) Euro Student 2000: Comparisons with the United Kingdom, in M. Slowey and D. Watson (eds.) *Higher Education and the Lifecourse*. Maidenhead: Society for Research into Higher Education and Open University Press.

Reeve, F., Cartwright, M. and Edwards, R. (eds.) (2002) *Supporting Lifelong Learning. Volume 2: Organizing Learning*. London: Routledge Falmer.

Reich, R. (2004) 'The Destruction of Public Higher Education in America, and How the UK Can Avoid the Same Fate'. Second Annual Higher Education Policy Institute Lecture, 25 March.

Richardson, J.T.E. (2004) *The National Student Survey: Final Report from the 2003 Pilot Project*. Institute of Educational Technology, Open University. (http:// iet.open.ac.uk/nss/download/hefce_report.pdf). Downloaded 27 July 2004.

Robson, B., Drake, K. and Deas, I. (1997) *National Committee of Inquiry into Higher Education Report 9, Higher Education and the Regions*. London: HMSO.

Romney, L.C., Bogen, G. and Micek, S.S. (1989) Assessing institutional performance: the importance of being careful, in M. Kogan (ed.) *Evaluating Higher Education*. London: Jessica Kingsley.

Rosenfield, R.H. and Wilson, D.C. (1999) *Managing Organizations, Texts, Readings and Cases*, 2nd edn. Maidenhead: McGraw-Hill.

RSM Robson Rhodes (2003) *Instituting Strategy: A Survey into the Use of Management Information in Promoting and Communicating Strategic Focus in Higher Education Institutions*. London: RSM Robson Rhodes.

Salford University (undated) *Salford University/CIHE Benchmarking of Academic Enterprise*. (www.upbeat.org.uk/downloads/project%20overviewa.pdf). Downloaded 27 July 2004.

Sallis, E. and Jones, J. (2002) *Knowledge Management in Education: Enhancing Learning and Education*. London: Kogan Page.

Saupe, J.L. (1990) *The Functions of Institutional Research*, 2nd edn. Tallahassee, FL: Association for Institutional Research. (http://www.airweb.org/page. asp?page=85). Downloaded 28 July 2004

Schoemaker, P.J.H. (1995) Scenario planning, a tool for strategic thinking. *Sloan Business Review*, Winter. Reprinted in Dyson, R.G. and O'Brien, F.A. (eds.) (1998) *Strategic Development*. Chichester: John Wiley.

Schuller, T., Preston, J., Hammond, C., Brassett-Grundy, A. and Bynner, J. (2004) *The Benefits of Learning: The Impact of Education and Health, Family Life and Social Capital*. London: Routledge Falmer.

Scott, P. (2003) Learning and lessons, in D. Warner and D. Palfreyman (eds) *Managing Crisis*. Maidenhead and Philadelphia, PA: Open University Press.

SFCFHE (Scottish Funding Councils for Further and Higher Education) (2003) *Aiming Further and Higher. Joint Corporate Plan 2003–06*. Edinburgh: SFCFHE.

Shattock, M. (2001) *University of Cambridge: Review of University Management and Governance Issues arising out of the CAPSA Project*, 5 November. (http://www.admin.cam.ac.uk/reporter/2001–02/weekly/5861/). Downloaded 28 July 2004.

Shattock, M. (2003a) *Managing Successful Universities*. Maidenhead: Society for Research into Higher Education and Open University Press.

Shattock, M. (2003b) Research, administration and university management: what can research contribute to policy?, in R. Begg (ed.) *The Dialogue Between Higher Education Research and Practice*. Dordrecht, Boston and London: Kluwer Academic Publishers.

Sizer, J. (1989) Institutional performance assessment under conditions of changing needs, in M. Kogan (ed.) *Evaluating Higher Education*. London: Jessica Kingsley.

Slack, N., Chambers, S. and Johnston, R. (2001) *Operations Management*, 3rd edn. Harlow: Pearson Education Limited.

Slovacek, S.P. (1988) Strategic planning and self-study, in H.R. Kells and F.A. van Vught (eds) *Self-Regulation, Self-Study and Program Review in Higher Education*. Culemborg, Netherlands: Lemma.

Slowey, M. (2003) Higher education and civil society, in M. Slowey and D. Watson (eds.) *Higher Education and the Lifecourse*. Buckingham: Society for Research into Higher Education and Open University Press.

Slowey, M. and Watson, D. (eds.) (2003) *Higher Education and the Lifecourse*.

Buckingham: Society for Research into Higher Education and Open University Press.

Sterling, M. (2002) 'Engineering – the Future: Or Engineering the Future'. Institute of Electrical Engineers Presidential Address, 3 October. (www.iee.org/TheIEE/President/PA02/index.cfm). Downloaded 29 July 2004.

Strydom, H.A., Lategan, L.O.K. and Muller, A. (eds.) (1997) *Enhancing Institutional Self-Evaluation and Quality in South African Higher Education: National and International Perspectives*. Bloemfontein: University of the Orange Free State.

Suslow, S. (1971) 'Present Reality of Institutional Research'. Presidential Address to the 11th Annual Forum, Association of Institutional Research. Quoted in McLaughlin, G. and Howard, R. (2001) Theory, practice and ethics of institutional research, in R. Howard (ed.) *Institutional Research: Decision Support in Higher Education*. Tallahassee, FL: Association for Institutional Research.

Thomas, H. (2001) *Managing Financial Resources*. Buckingham and Philadelphia, PA: Open University Press.

Tight, M. (2003) *Researching Higher Education*. Buckingham: Society for Research into Higher Education and Open University Press.

UNITE (2003) *Student Living Report 2003*. Bristol: UNITE.

UNITE (2004) *Student Living Report 2004*. Bristol: UNITE

University of Edinburgh (2004) *Balanced Scorecard Overview*. (http://www.planning.ed.ac.uk/BSC/why.htm). Downloaded 14 July 2004.

UUK (Universities UK) (2001a) *Patterns of Higher Education Institutions in the UK: First Report*. London: UUK.

UUK (2001b) *The Regional Mission. The Regional Contribution of Higher Education. The South East*. London: UUK.

UUK (2002) *Patterns of Higher Education Institutions in the UK: Second Report*. London: UUK.

UUK (2003) *Patterns of Higher Education Institutions in the UK: Third Report*. London: UUK.

UUK (2004) *Putting the HE in Health*. Report of a seminar of the Longer Term Strategy Group and Health Committee, April (unpublished).

van der Heijden, K. (1996) *Scenarios, the Art of Strategic Conversation*. Chichester: John Wiley.

van der Heijden, K. (1997) *Scenarios, Strategies and the Strategy Process*. Breuken: Nijenrode University Press.

Volkwein, J.F. (1999) *What Is Institutional Research All About? A Critical and Comprehensive Assessment of the Profession*. San Francisco, CA: Jossey-Bass.

Warner, D. and Palfreyman, D. (2003) Setting the scene, in D. Warner and D. Palfreyman (eds) *Managing Crisis*. Maidenhead and Philadelphia, PA: Open University Press.

Warner, D. and Palfreyman, D. (eds) (2003) *Managing Crisis*. Maidenhead and Philadelphia: Open University Press.

Watson, D. (2000) *Managing Strategy*. Buckingham and Philadelphia, PA: Open University Press.

Watson, D. (2003a) Research intensity: a new university perspective, in *The UK Higher Education Research Yearbook*. Leeds: Evidence Ltd.

Watson, D. (2003b) The university and life chances, in M. Slowey and D. Watson (eds.) *Higher Education and the Lifecourse*. Maidenhead: Society for Research into Higher Education and Open University Press.

Watson, D. (2004) *ACU Benchmarking Programme 2004: The University and Civic Engagement*. (www.brighton.ac.uk/cupp/word%20files/bench_dev.doc). Downloaded 30 July 2004.

Watson, D. and Bowden, R. (1999) Now look at our figures. *Guardian Higher*, 9 November: 2–3.

Watson, D. and Bowden, R. (2002) *The New University Decade, 1992–2002*. University of Brighton Education Research Centre Occasional Paper.

Watson, D. and Taylor, R. (1998) *Lifelong Learning and the University: A Post-Dearing Agenda*. London: Falmer Press.

Watson, G.H. (1993) *Strategic Benchmarking*. New York, NY: Wiley.

Whittington, R. (1993) *What is Strategy and Does It Matter?* London: International Thompson Business Press.

Wissema, H. (2002) Driving through red lights: how warning signals are missed or ignored. *Long Range Planning*, 35(5): 521–39.

Yorke, M. (1991) *Performance Indicators: Observations on Their Use in the Assurance of Course Quality*. London: Council for National Academic Awards.

Yorke, M. (2004) Institutional research and its relevance to the performance of higher education institutions. *Journal of Higher Education Policy and Management*, 26(2): 141–52.

Žižek, S. (2004) Between two deaths, *London Review of Books*, 3 June.

APPENDIX 1

UNIVERSITY OF BRIGHTON REPORTS AND DOCUMENTS

(2001a) *Personnel Department Information Bulletin Issue No. 7* (Reported Sickness Absence). Unpublished.

(2001b) *Main Points Raised in the Participation Profile of the University of Brighton* (Matieu Hiely-Rayner, Strategic Planning Unit. Unpublished).

(2001c) *University Perception Survey 2001* (Matieu Hiely-Rayner, Strategic Planning Unit. Unpublished).

(2002a) *Undergraduate Retention 1999/00 to 2000/01* (Stephan Butler and Matieu Hiely-Rayner. Unpublished).

(2002b) *Why Students Choose the University of Brighton*. Report of the survey of first year students' attitudes in September 2002 (Statistics Consultancy Unit. Unpublished).

(2002c) *Effectiveness of the Board* (Board Paper B/45/02. Unpublished).

(2002d) *Undergraduate Retention 2000/01 to 2001/02* (Stephan Butler and Matieu Hiely-Rayner. Unpublished).

(2003a) *Corporate Plan 2002–07*. Brighton: University of Brighton.

(2003b) *Competitor Analysis of Comparator Group for 2002 Entry* (Matieu Hiely-Rayner, Strategic Planning Unit. Unpublished).

(2003c) *Commercial Strategy* (unpublished).

(2003d) *Why Students Choose the University of Brighton: Report on the Survey of First Year Students' Attitudes, 2002*. Brighton: Statistics Consultancy Unit, University of Brighton.

(2003e) *Why Students Choose the University of Brighton: Comparison Report of 1998 and 2002*. Brighton: Statistics Consultancy Unit, University of Brighton.

(2003f) *Alumni Survey* (Marketing and Communications Department. Unpublished).

(2003g) *The Financial Situation of Students at the University of Brighton: The Twelfth Report 2003–04* by Sarah Pemberton and Sandra Winn, Health and Social Policy Research Centre. Brighton: University of Brighton.

(2003h) *The Experiences of New Lecturers at the University of Brighton* (Joyce

Barlow and Maria Antoniou, Centre for Learning and Teaching. Unpublished).

(2003i) *Institutional Approaches to Improving Student Success at the University of Brighton* (Rachel Bowden, Strategic Planning Unit. Unpublished).

(2003j) *Minutes of the Academic Standards Committee, 16 December* (unpublished).

(2003k) *Processes of Studentification in Brighton and Eastbourne* (Darren P. Smith and Louise Holt, School of the Environment. Unpublished).

(2003l) *Customer Satisfaction Survey: Catering Services* (Residential and Catering Services. Unpublished).

(2003m) *Academic Appeals: Report from the Secretary to Academic Board*, AB03–70, December (unpublished).

(2004a) *Self-evaluation Document* (unpublished).

(2004b) *Undergraduate Prospectus 2005*. Brighton: University of Brighton.

(2004c) *Undergraduate Retention, 2002/03 to 2003/04* (Matieu Hiely-Rayner, Strategic Planning Unit. Unpublished).

(2004d) *Why Students Choose the University of Brighton* and the *Decliners' Survey*. Brighton: Statistics Consultancy Unit, University of Brighton.

(2004e) *Corporate Plan – Evaluating Performance*. Board of Governors B/42/04, June (unpublished).

(2004f) *Research Strategy*. Brighton: University of Brighton.

(2004g) *Report on the Withdrawal Survey October 2003–April 2004*. Student Retention Review Group, May (unpublished).

(2004h) *Information Services Survey of Users* (Information Services. Unpublished).

(2004i) *Management Information Report for the Eleven Months to June 2004, 2003–04 financial year* (unpublished).

Other University of Brighton publications

Azure Consulting International (2003) *Organisational Character Index Report* (unpublished consultancy report).

Cooper, C. (2001) *Work-life Balance Survey* (Robertson Cooper Ltd. (Unpublished Consultancy report).

University of Brighton Students' Union (2004) *Student Written Submission* (unpublished).

Watson, D. (2002) 'Self-study and University Strategy: Keynote Speech for the Education Research Centre Conference: Relevance and Diversity'. University of Brighton, 31 May.

Webb, H. (1998) *How Should Universities Change Their Resource Provision to Meet the Needs of an Increasingly Diverse Student Population?* Unpublished MBA thesis, University of Brighton.

APPENDIX 2

WEBSITES REFERRED TO IN THE TEXT (CORRECT AS AT JULY 2004)

Organizations

www.acu.ac.uk – Association of Commonwealth Universities (ACU). Includes links to the ACU programme on benchmarking university management.

http://airweb.org – US Association for Institutional Research (AIR).

www.balancedscorecard.org – the Balanced Scorecard Institute (USA). Contains basic information about the model and links to organizations that use it, including some universities.

www.eair.com – European Association for Institutional Research (EAIR).

www.evidencenetwork.org – Economic and Social Research Council (ESRC) UK Centre for Evidence-based Policy and Practice.

www.hefce.ac.uk – Higher Education Funding Council for England (HEFCE), including electronic access to HEFCE publications.

www.hepi.ac.uk – Higher Education Policy Institute (HEPI), including electronic access to discussion and policy papers produced by HEPI.

www.hero.ac.uk – web portal for information on UK higher education, including increasingly about quality, for students and other stakeholders.

www.hesa.ac.uk – Higher Education Statistics Agency (HESA), including information on data collections, analytical services and some online data.

http://iet.open.ac.uk/nss/ – National Student Survey (NSS), including electronic access to reports about the NSS project.

www.ltsn.ac.uk/genericcentre/index.asp – Learning and Teaching Support Network (LTSN) generic centre site with links to documents on evidence-based practice and the *Network for Institutional Researchers*. Now part of the HE Academy.

www.oecd.ord/edu/higher – the programme on *Institutional Management in Higher Education*.

www.qaa.ac.uk – the Quality Assurance Agency for Higher Education (QAA), including institutional audit reports.

www.quality.nist.gov/ – the Baldrige National Quality Program.

www.scup.org – US Society of College and University Planning (SCUP). Much, but not all, of this is about planning the institutional estate.

www.strategy.gov.uk – Strategy Unit within the Cabinet Office. Site includes comprehensive advice about strategizing, futures work and risk management in government.

www.tomorrowproject.net – the Tomorrow Project. Information on aspects of future policy issues in the UK.

Selected higher education institution self-study and project sites

www.brighton.ac.uk – University of Brighton, including electronic access to some of the publications referred to in the text.

www.cupp.org.uk – Community University Partnership Project at the University of Brighton, including links to benchmarking for community engagement.

www.effectingchange.luton.ac.uk – project about leading change in higher education, funded under the HEFCE Good Management Practice initiative.

www.imir.iupui.edu – Indiana University/Purdue University Office of Institutional Management and Institutional Research

www.iport.iupui.edu/selfstudy – Indiana University/Purdue University Indiana self-study for accreditation.

www.ir.ufl.edu.mups – University of Florida self-study.

www.pitar.co.uk – *Programme Improvement Through Alumni Research Project*, funded under the HEFCE Good Management Practice initiative.

www.planning.ed.ac.uk – the Planning Section at the University of Edinburgh, including information on applying the balanced scorecard to university performance.

www.port.edu/selfstudy – Indiana University/Purdue University Indiana self-study.

www.thecenter.ufl.edu – *The Center*, hosting the Lombardi Program on Measuring University Performance, based at the University of Florida.

www.udd.edu/IR/cost/ – University of Delaware/National Study of Institutional Costs and Productivity.

www.upbeat.org.uk – University of Salford-led project to identify indicators for university/community engagement, funded by the Council for Industry and Higher Education (CIHE), Higher Education Funding Council for England (HEFCE) and the Engineering and Physical Sciences Research Council (EPSRC).

INDEX

EDUCATIONAL DEVELOPMENT
Discourse, Identity and Practice

Ray Land

- What do educational developers see as the main issues to be tackled within their work?
- How does the educational context and culture in which they work affect the practice of educational developers?
- How do educational developers perceive change occurring within higher education organizations?

In higher education institutions worldwide, issues relating to quality in teaching and learning have gained prominence over the last two decades as student numbers, and the need to be publicly accountable, have increased. During this time a sizeable community of educational developers has emerged whose work and research focuses on the enhancement of the student experience in higher education. A significant issue for these developers is how change can be effected in organizations with well-established academic cultures and practices, beset by many other priorities and pressures.

This first book-length analysis of developers as a community of practice illustrates in their own words the issues they face, their differing orientations to development (given their differing organizational cultures), and how they see their institutional role. What emerges is the contested notion of 'development' itself, and a tribe of developers who, though fragmented, offer a rich variation in their discourse, identity and practice.

Drawing upon developers' own voices, the book offers a lively and accessible narrative approach to this rapidly evolving area. It is a useful guide to help individual developers compare their own practice with that of others, and development teams to map the effectiveness of their own centre's provision.

Educational Development is essential reading for educational developers, teaching and learning co-ordinators and teaching fellows, as well as senior managers with remits for academic development, and directors of quality assurance. It is also of interest to those in higher education who are concerned with bringing about organizational or cultural change.

Contents:

232pp   0 335 21328 6 (Paperback)   0 335 21329 4 (Hardback)

MANAGING CRISIS
David Warner and David Palfreyman

- Why do crises arise in further and higher education institutions?
- How can these crises be overcome?
- What lessons can be learnt?

There have been several high profile crises in higher education during the last two decades. *Managing Crisis* draws together a number of senior academic managers to prepare, probably for the first time ever, a series of detailed institutional case-studies. These case-studies identify the nature of the crisis, describe the action taken to resolve it, and consider the lasting consequences. An important chapter gives the informed perspectives of the funding council on higher education crises, and in the final chapter the inimitable Peter Scott draws a series of significant conclusions.

Managing Crisis is the first book to examine crises in higher education in detail and to identify key points on how to overcome or avoid them. Required reading for managers working within UK Higher Education Policy.

Contents
Foreword – Notes on contributors – List of abbreviations – Setting the scene – Crisis at Cardiff – Capital building and cash flow at the University of Lancaster – How one man wove a kind of magic in Ealing – Southampton Institute – The experience of London Guildhall University – Heartbreak ending for a foreign affair – The Lambeth hike – A Funding Council perspective – Learning the lessons – References – Index.

Contributors
Roger Brown, Vanessa Cunningham, Chris Duke, Sir Brian Fender, Roderick Floud, Lucy Hodges, Marion McClintock, David Palfreyman, Adrian Perry, William Richie, Peter Scott, Sir Brian Smith, Sir William Taylor, David Warner.

216pp   0 335 21058 9 (Paperback)   0 335 21059 7 (Hardback)

MANAGING STRATEGY
David Watson

Higher education institutions are under increasing pressure to produce corporate and strategic plans, both for external audiences (such as funding bodies and other 'partners') and for the internal purposes of setting and achieving goals. They are significantly dependent upon public investment and the expectations of public bodies as well as upon a fast-changing market for their products and services.

David Watson sets out what strategic management can and should consist of in a modern, essentially democratic, university or college, and how to make it work. He examines for instance:

- how universities and colleges should go about satisfying legitimate external and internal requirements for their corporate plans
- how they should maximize their strategic assets and opportunities, and minimize their weaknesses and threats
- the role of governance and management in setting and achieving a strategic plan

This book demonstrates how the academy has to adapt to meet the needs of its rapidly changing host society as well as of a more diverse and plural internal community, whilst maintaining a range of historical commitments. The result is an account of strategic management that is simultaneously careful of traditional values, restorative of those that have fallen into abeyance, and genuinely innovative.

Contents

176pp   0 335 20345 0 (Paperback)   0 335 20346 9 (Hardback)

MANAGING SUCCESSFUL UNIVERSITIES
Michael Shattock

"Michael Shattock is the master craftsman of sturdy self-reliance in modern public universities. Knowing that ministerial steering will not, can not, do the job in the twenty-first century, he charts an alternative course for continuous change. His liberating lessons will be useful not only in Britain but around the world."
Professor Burton R. Clark, University of California, Los Angeles

"...this important new book strengthens the argument for seeing good management as a necessary condition for effective and worthwhile teaching, learning and research, and its neglect as a serious threat to core academic values."
Professor Sir William Taylor, Former Director,
University of London Institute of Education

"Michael Shattock is without doubt Britain's leading authority on the dangerously neglected subject of university management...For some his book will not make comfortable reading."
Professor Geoffrey Alderman, Vice-President, American Inter-
Continental University, London

This book seeks to define good management in a university context and how it can contribute to university success. It emphasizes the holistic characteristics of university management, the need to be outward looking and entrepreneurial in management style, the importance of maintaining a strong academic/administrative part-nership and a continuous dialogue between the centre and academic departments, and the preservation of a self-directed institutional autonomy. It draws on the literature of management in the private sector as well as from higher education, and from the experience of the author. *Managing Successful Universities* demonstrates how successful universities utilize the market to reinforce academic excellence.

Contents
Introduction – What are the characteristics of a successful uni-versity? – Strategic management in universities – Managing uni-versity finance – The academic context: Organization, collegiality and leadership – Good governance – Extending the boundaries – Building an image, establishing a reputation – Ambition – Inhibi-tions to becoming entrepreneurial – Turning round failure or arresting decline – Managing universities for success – Appendix – References – Index.

216pp   0 335 20961 0 (Paperback)   0 335 20962 9 (Hardback)

RETENTION AND STUDENT SUCCESS IN HIGHER EDUCATION
Mantz Yorke and Bernard Longden

- What is the policy background to current interest in retention and student success?
- What causes students to leave institutions without completing their programmes?
- How can theory and research help institutions to encourage student success?

Retention and completion rates are important measures of the performance of institutions and higher education systems. Understanding the causes of student non-completion is vital for an institution seeking to increase the chances of student success.

The early chapters of this book discuss retention and student success from a public policy perspective. The later chapters concentrate on theory and research evidence, and on how these can inform institutional practices designed to enhance retention and success (particularly where students are enrolled from disadvantaged backgrounds).

This book draws upon international experience, particularly from the United Kingdom, Australia, South Africa and the United States.

Retention and Student Success in Higher Education is essential reading for lecturers, support staff, and senior managers in higher education institutions, and for those with a wider policy interest in these matters.

Contents

200pp   0 335 21274 3 (Paperback)   0 335 21275 1 (Hardback)